Margaret Irvin Carrington

Ab-sa-ra-ka, Home of the Crows

Being the Experience of an Officer's Wife on the Plains

Margaret Irvin Carrington

Ab-sa-ra-ka, Home of the Crows
Being the Experience of an Officer's Wife on the Plains

ISBN/EAN: 9783337145392

Printed in Europe, USA, Canada, Australia, Japan

Cover: Foto ©ninafisch / pixelio.de

More available books at **www.hansebooks.com**

AB-SA-RA-KA

HOME OF THE CROWS:

BEING THE

EXPERIENCE OF AN OFFICER'S WIFE

ON

THE PLAINS,

AND

MARKING THE VICISSITUDES OF PERIL AND PLEASURE
DURING THE OCCUPATION OF THE NEW ROUTE TO VIRGINIA
CITY, MONTANA, 1866-7, AND THE INDIAN HOSTILITY THERETO·

WITH

OUTLINES OF THE NATURAL FEATURES AND RESOURCES OF THE
LAND, TABLES OF DISTANCES, MAPS, AND OTHER AIDS TO
THE TRAVELER; GATHERED FROM OBSERVATION
AND OTHER RELIABLE SOURCES.

PHILADELPHIA:
J. B. LIPPINCOTT & CO.
1869.

DEDICATION.

WITH acknowledgments to LIEUTENANT-GENERAL SHERMAN, whose suggestions at Fort Kearney, in the spring of 1866, were adopted, in preserving a daily record of the events of a peculiarly eventful journey, and whose vigorous policy is as promising of the final settlement of Indian troubles and the quick completion of the Union Pacific Railroad as his *"March to the Sea"* was signal in crushing the last hope of armed rebellion, this narrative is respectfully dedicated.

MARGARET IRVIN CARRINGTON.

ILLUSTRATIONS.

MAP.

	PAGE
COURT-HOUSE ROCK	67
CHIMNEY ROCK	68
CAMP PHISTERER CANON	84
EAST VIEW OF NORTH PLATTE, NEAR SAGE CREEK	86
LARAMIE PEAK, FROM THE NORTH	89
FORT PHIL KEARNEY	147
SURROUNDINGS OF FORT PHIL KEARNEY	204

CONTENTS.

CHAPTER I.
                                                                       PAGE

Absaraka, Home of the Crows 13

CHAPTER II.
Absaraka described.. 20

CHAPTER III.
The Natural History and Climate of Absaraka............... 29

CHAPTER IV.
Organization of the Expedition to Absaraka................. 36

CHAPTER V.
From Fort Kearney to crossing of Union Pacific Railroad—Incidents of the Platte River Travel—Reunion of the Officers of the 18th Infantry—Crossing the Ridiculous Platte.. 45

CHAPTER VI.
Reminiscences of Ranching, and old times on the route from Leavenworth to Sedgwick.................................... 55

CHAPTER VII.
Union Pacific Railroad to Laramie—Court-house Rock—Chimney Rock—Fortification Rock—Scott's Bluffs—Wonderful Fishing—Visit of Standing Elk............... 64

CHAPTER VIII.

Fort Laramie Council of 1866—Its results foreshadowed—The Aborigines in the marts of trade—How the Indians did and did not 73

CHAPTER IX.

Laramie to Reno—Camp Phisterer Cañon—Laramie Peak—Wild Flora—Pumpkin Buttes 82

CHAPTER X.

Fort Reno—Indian Raid—Fort Laramie Treaty tested—Fourth of July in Absaraka—Organization of Mountain District—Onward Movement—More Rattlesnakes—Mercury 113° above zero—What it did 93

CHAPTER XI.

Reconnoissances—Indian messengers—Warnings—Location of Fort Philip Kearney—Conduct of the troops, and its cause 102

CHAPTER XII.

Arrival of Indians—The Cheyennes in council—Black Horse, The Rabbit that Jumps, Red Sleeve, Dull Knife, and others have much talk and "heap of smoke" 110

CHAPTER XIII.

Massacre of Louis Gazzou's party—Indian raid and great loss of mules—The Cheyennes again—Forty hostile demonstrations of the "peaceable tribes"—The Laramie Treaty incidentally tested—Massacre of Lieutenant Daniels—A fighting parson 119

CHAPTER XIV.

Conduct of the Crow Indians—What Bridger and Beckwith say 139

CHAPTER XV.

Visit of Inspector-General Hazen — Reinforcements on the way—Mounted Infantry compared with Sioux Light Cavalry—United States mails—Corral system—Timber and lumber supplied to order...................................... 134

CHAPTER XVI.

Fort Philip Kearney and surroundings—A picnic—Ascent of the mountains—Lake Smedt—Fine scenery—Plan of the fort.. 141

CHAPTER XVII.

Two holidays—October inspection and review—First garrison flag hoisted in Absaraka—Incidents of the day—Indian response to a national salute—Looking-glasses in abundance—Evening levee.. 150

CHAPTER XVIII.

A day of incidents—Hostile Sioux and friendly Cheyennes—Narrow escape of the latter—Our picket mimicked—More massacres—Croquet introduced into Absaraka.. 157

CHAPTER XIX.

Night scenes—Celestial and terrestrial visitors—Aurora—Lunar rainbow—Meteorites—Indians all in their war-paint.. 164

CHAPTER XX.

Domestic, social, and religious life, with the episodes therein occurring.. 173

CHAPTER XXI.

Indian warfare—Things a woman can learn when she has seen them tried.. 180

CHAPTER XXII.
Indian arms, habits, and customs—The arrow beats the revolver.. 187

CHAPTER XXIII.
Massacre of Lieutenant Bingham—Accounts given by officers—Extracts from journal................................. 194

CHAPTER XXIV.
Fetterman's massacre—Its lessons................................ 200

CHAPTER XXV.
The funeral—Burial of fourscore and one victims of the massacre—Cold and sad holidays—Expeditions abandoned—Reinforcements of August yet behind............ 211

CHAPTER XXVI.
Comedy of errors—Enterprise of the press—Transactions in Absaraka mysteriously known to the public before they had information of the same................................ 218

CHAPTER XXVII.
New Year's changes—1867—March to Fort Reno—Mercury 40° below zero—How it felt and what it did........ 226

CHAPTER XXVIII.
Fort Reno to Fort Caspar—Thence to the United States—Courtesies of the route—Visits of dignitaries, military, civil, and Indian, at McPherson—More changes.. 237

CHAPTER XXIX.
In memoriam... 244

CHAPTER XXX.
Omaha to Virginia City, Montana............................... 250

APPENDIX I.. 259
APPENDIX II... 270

PROLOGUE.

THE importunity of friends, who have been interested in the journal of a summer's trip and a winter's experience on the Plains, and which, as a matter of taste, now assumes the more easy flow of Narrative, has overruled the first refusal to permit its use in more available form for their leisurely reading. Gathering many of its details from officers of the posts, from Major James Bridger, and others, and so gathering as each day's experience unfolded events of interest, there is no assumption of anything further than to express the facts so recorded just as they were impressed upon the judgment or fancy.

If, on the one hand, the recital of military preparations or movements be so inartificial as to excite the smile of the critic, or if the natural tendency to adopt the idioms and style which, every way and forever, surround the wife of an officer, shall seem so constrained as to repel the lady reader, it can only be said that we wrote, when we wrote, just as the surroundings inspired or compelled us.

In this change from the form of a journal we have adhered to its record, and preserved the integrity of the original, so as to reproduce our life as it was lived and give incidents as they transpired.

While nearly one-half of the Indian demonstrations were under our own eye, the authentic reports of others were of equal value to history; and the narrative differs little from what would be the written experience of others, except that we availed ourselves more fully of classes of facts and sources of knowledge equally open to all, and so cherished their record, as in earlier life we garnered up details of a first visit to Mammoth Cave or the Falls of Niagara.

If our statistics and statements as to Indian councils, usages, or raids, or the record of labor, casualties, and incidents, savor much of *routine*, yet through incidental form we have gathered historical facts, and thus do we present our life and the exact history of the first year of the military occupation of Absaraka.

And again; if there be a savor of whining because the soldiers were so few and support was unfurnished, it will not be taken as criticism to offend anybody, since everybody knows how small was the army, and how incapable of immediate expansion to meet the issues of the Northwestern frontier at the close of the war.

So, then, our friends will accept this response to their wishes, and *at least* gather instruction for their guidance when they undertake their first visit to Absaraka, Home of the Crows.

AB-SA-RA-KA.

CHAPTER I.

ABSARAKA, HOME OF THE CROWS.

ABSARAKA, in the language of the Crow Indians, translated, *Home of the Crows*, was once the field of their proudest successes.

The fertile basins of the Yellowstone, Big Horn, and Tongue Rivers were enlivened by the presence of their many villages; and in the early days of Bridger and Beckwith, the Crow Indians accumulated considerable wealth by a prolific trade in pelts and dressed furs, which those veteran trappers and frontiersmen delivered for them at St. Louis and other border depots for Indian commerce.

Partially girt in by the Big Horn and Panther Mountains, yet roaming at will, they were masters of a region of country which has no peer in its exhaustless game resources, and is rarely surpassed in its production of wild fruits, grasses, and cereals; while its natural scenery, made up of snowy crests, pine-clad slopes and summits, crystal waters, and luxuriant vales, certainly has no rival in our great sisterhood of States.

The Snake Indians, who roamed farther north and west, and who had even crossed lances with the Pagans and Bloods, on the confines of British America, were unable, man for man, to match their more numerous and more adventurous rivals, the Crows, and at last, in 1856, joined friendly hands with them, or at least observed a fair neutrality in the later conflicts of the Crows with their hereditary and deadly enemies, the Sioux and Northern Cheyennes.

When the Cheyennes of the Black Hills of Eastern Dakota divided their bands, and one portion went to the Red River country, while another portion left the old home, with nearly half of the remaining families, for Powder River and Tongue River valleys, the Ogillalla Sioux at last found allies to support their operations against the Crows. With a portion of the Arrapahoes, Blackfeet, and Gros Ventres of the Prairie, popularly known as the Big Bellies, they prosecuted the war with vigor and unrelenting hatred. Breaking into the long-coveted region about which they had been testing their valor for years in fruitless forays and uncertain adventures, the Sioux, aided by their new friends, succeeded in occupying the choice valleys of the lower Big Horn and Tongue Rivers, and still held them in comparative independence when the expedition of 1866, sent to open the new route to Virginia City, forced them to accept the challenge of the *white man* for the future possession of their stolen dwelling-place.

The Crows fell back of the Yellowstone, though still operating eastward as far as the west bank of Big Horn River; and a few attempted something like local improvement, imitating the Flat Heads, who, though few of numbers, were not the less energetic, and seemed to be really desirous of gaining some affinity with the ideas and civilization of the whites.

With all these changes and the continued aggression of the Sioux, the Crows maintained their passion for their old and their favorite home. It had its peculiar virtues. At once grand and beautiful, prolific in game beyond all precedent, susceptible of culture and the development of vast mineral wealth, while offering a new avenue for travel to Montana nearly five hundred miles shorter than that by Salt Lake City, how can it be deemed strange that they looked upon that redundancy of game, that exceeding fertility, and that natural forage, as wonderfully adapted for their perpetual home and abiding-place!

The white man had given it no distinctive

name, and had scarcely trespassed upon its soil. Farther west, he had occupied the Madison and Jefferson branches and the head waters of the Missouri. Flourishing towns and cities had been located, and the Indians, who had so long been driven westward, were *now* crowded *back* upon the Yellowstone and Big Horn; so that the Crows must soon renew their active antagonism with their old plunderers, or seek other fields or methods of life.

This great hunting sphere, though nameless, had a natural independence both of Montana and Dakota, while attached in part to each. All that lies east of Black Foot and Clarke's Passes had its special relation to the territory extending as far as Powder River. Somebody had indeed ventured to style this country *Wyoming*, a name which might do very well for a county of Pennsylvania, but had the least claim for application to the stolen land of the Crows.

These same Crow Indians, in addition to their natural title to the land, maintain, to this day, the proud claim *never to have killed a white man but in self-defense*. All their intercourse in 1866, and their relations in 1867, combine to show the integrity of their friendship and the truth of their protestations.

Their very enemies concede to them the rightful title to the territory so long struggled for.

At a formal council held at Fort Philip Kearney in July, 1866, between Colonel Carrington and certain Cheyenne chiefs, who were then in close relations with Red Cloud and other *Ogillalla* Sioux, but desirous of breaking loose from the tie, that they might receive protection from the whites, the following question was addressed to Black Horse:

"*Why do the Sioux and Cheyennes claim the land which belongs to the Crows?*"

Black Horse, The Wolf that Lies Down, Red Arm, and Dull Knife promptly answered:

"*The Sioux helped us. We stole the hunting-grounds of the Crows because they were the best. The white man is along the great waters, and we wanted more room. We fight the Crows, because they will not take half and give us peace with the other half.*"

Absaraka is therefore in fact, as the Crows have fondly named that whole region (absurdly styled Wyoming by some), the "Home of the Crows."

Bound to it by sacred legends; endeared as it is by years of occupation and wasting conflicts for its repossession; pressed by the whites from the west, and now approached from the east, yet restricted to the use of the Upper Yellowstone and west bank of the Big Horn Rivers, the Crows still maintain their rightful title, and ask of the white man that he acknowledge it.

No less firmly do they maintain inviolate their

2*

solemn faith once pledged to the white man, and they look to his advent, in sufficient numbers, as the signal of their own deliverance and the destruction of their old enemies the Sioux.

Ready to co-operate with the whites—*kindly disposed toward the new road*—beginning to appreciate the fate of the red man who shall oppose the progress of civilization and frontier settlement, they regard with something like hope the strong arm of that progress, and stand ready to perpetuate their own life by a just conformity to its reasonable demands.

There is another fact which appeals strongly to other sentiments than those that favor simple justice.

Among all the tribes of the Northwest, the Crow Indian stands *first* in manliness and physical perfection.

While they alone have the title to negotiate the right of way for the New Virginia City road, independently of its *occupation* by the Sioux and their allies, they also have pride of race and nation. *They can be trusted as friends within its boundaries* whenever they are treated with the consideration they deserve. Would white men do more?

The Crows lost possession by robbery. Their enemies have become the white man's enemy. Their enemies have ignored treaty obligations, nave despised all terms of compromise or honorable warfare, and defy the Crows and white man alike.

To the Crow, therefore, should be tendered support and friendship. Whatever the result as to the possession of the soil, it is as wicked to give it to the Sioux, for fear of his enmity, as it is to rob the Crows, if they wish to retain or jointly enjoy it.

Above all, the land should bear its true name, and thus give to posterity *some* index to its past history and the issues and struggles which have preceded its use by the white man. Let it be known, whether as Territory, State, or Indian Reservation, as ABSARAKA, Home of the Crows.

Herein, honor is rendered to noble red men, for such these are! *Herein*, justice is done to the Crow nation, which has hardly been less honorable and true to their friendship than the Naragansetts, the Delawares, and the Pawnees. *Herein*, shall be established a memorial name that will connect with the last supremacy of the red man a tribute to those who were truly worthy; and past injustice shall be partially atoned for, in giving to the Crow Indians this perpetual recognition in the land of ABSARAKA, the Home of the Crows.

CHAPTER II.

ABSARAKA DESCRIBED.

THIS land of the largest liberty for the red man and the chase is as varied in surface and general features as it is attractive to the various tribes that have contended for its possession.

Nearly all maps, and even the experience of Major James Bridger, the chief guide of the expedition of 1866, and that of Mr. Brannan, an assistant guide, who was with General Connor in 1865, so far as he advanced in the valley of Tongue River, fail to furnish such data as to afford an adequate judgment of this region and its capacity for future development.

All guides and scouts very naturally fix their attention upon points where water and grazing can be found by emigrants *in transitu;* but they do not as often generalize the result of these varied adventures, and fix the relations of diverse soils and geographical features to the purposes of advancing civilization and general settlement.

And yet, as the army and people have been released from the engrossing interests of a great domestic war, and the failure of the Laramie treaty of 1866, with its immediate succession of hostilities to every foot of progress over the route claimed to have been guaranteed by that treaty, have turned the attention of the national Congress and the national army to this new field of fight, it will be found that no portion of the public domain, heretofore almost *terra-incognita*, will challenge a greater public favor when its elements of value are known.

Not that it will prove a paradise for mere adventurers who aspire after good and sudden riches at the expense of the substantial development of the lands they traverse and prospect; but this idea is founded upon the basis of actual settlement, and the ultimate adoption of Absaraka into the great family of American States.

And yet, it is true that even the adventurer will find a field of promise. Every creek, from Clear Fork to the Upper Yellowstone, gives gold color, and there is no doubt that patient, well-directed labor will realize fair returns. Certain it is, that but for the Indian hostilities—engendered partly by bad faith exercised toward some of their bands; partly by excessive intimacy, degrading to both the white and red man, and resulting in the ultimate vengeance of the latter when he learns the drift of such intimacy; partly by failure to support the Indians who deserve support; and especially by failure to punish those who were incorrigibly wicked and ugly—the new route, so short, and in the main so fruitful in supplies for the emigrant, would become a favorite with all travelers to Eastern and Lower Montana.

Of course it has its supposed rivals. SALT LAKE CITY, so beautiful in location, with its shaded avenues, its ever-flowing fountains, and lavish soil, cannot cheerfully spare from its markets the long trains which have made the circuit by its route; and everybody who owns a light-draught steamer will willingly transport from St. Louis, Nebraska City, or Omaha, as many passengers as the capacity of his cabin or the stage of river moisture will permit; but the mathematical difficulty of making the hypothenuse of an acute angled triangle greater than the sum of the sides is a never-failing embarrassment to either party, and the question of distance remains as nature established it.

The honest stranger who seeks a home in Lower Montana, and a short reliable route to Bozeman City, the Gallatin Valley, and Jefferson City, and the agricultural or mineral districts of that region, desires more definite information of the land to which his thoughts turn; and not only the people of Nebraska, Iowa, Minnesota, Illinois, and Indiana, but those of more eastern States, are pushing their trains across the plains, looking in vain, as they have long looked, for some definite details of the route they are to traverse.

It is not always convenient, each day, for the

emigrant to depend upon some transient ranchero or squatter for information as to the next grass, timber, or water along the route; and it is therefore of practical value for the traveler to have a definite outline of the country before furnishing such details as specify the route, with its history, resources, and supplies.

The *geographical* outline of Absaraka is special and full of interest.

The general course of the Big Horn Mountains is from southeast to northwest, until it reaches the Big Horn River, when the direction changes westward; but the Big Horn Mountains proper die out before reaching the Upper Yellowstone River and Clark's and Blackfoot Passes, yet only a short distance from the former.

At the lower or southeastern terminus, the range doubles back upon itself to the southwest, in form not unlike a BIG HORN or cornucopia, and gives significance to its name, although the "Big Horn" of the mountain sheep is credited as source of the title.

Of course it is presumed that the reader has gained some knowledge of the course of the Platte, and entertains at least general ideas of the routes to Salt Lake City by way of Denver, Fort Bridger, or Forts Laramie and Caspar.

While this narrative will embrace directions for the traveler, even from the South Platte, and especially after the journey leaves the line of the

Union Pacific Railroad, with all the definiteness needed for daily practical use, it does not require, in this general description of Absaraka, that those elements should be noticed at present.

Omitting, therefore, all branches of the Big Cheyenne, and all tributaries of either Fork of the Platte, the general survey begins with Powder River.

Powder River, which is a muddy stream, comes from the southern side of the Big Horn Mountains and a southwestern source, and therefore is not a part of the great aggregate of bright channels that combine to feed the Missouri River from the Big Horn range proper. True it is, that it may be held responsible for their subsequent discoloration, and it does help the Missouri to no little portion of that final burden of deposit and gravity which so unfavorably appeals to the first taste of the traveler from the East; but this is *its mission*, and simply vindicates its own character, as do similar currents in the aggregate of the great flow of human life.

The Big Horn range of the Rocky Mountains possesses two distinct and marked features. There is, first, a central or backbone range, which culminates in perpetual snow, where Cloud Peak grandly rises as the chief of all its proud summits, falling off slowly and patiently toward the southern valleys that are soon confronted by similar ranges of the Wind River Mountains beyond.

The second range is north of the first, and after clearly leaving the loftier sweep, it presents nearly a perpendicular face to the north, except where the earnest torrents have cut deep gorges, and thus forced their way to the main tributaries of the Missouri.

Between these ranges, and varying in breadth from twelve to twenty-five miles, are fine hunting-grounds, abounding in noble orchards, wild fruits and grasses, as well as the choicest game for the huntsman. This special tract is hardly a true plateau, as are the more uniform offsets of the *Tierre Calients* of the Mexican ranges; but with all its vicinity to perpetual snow, there are gentle slopes which possess peculiar loveliness and many elements of future value. With this general outline in mind, let the traveler start from Fort Reno on Powder River.

He is in the midst of a sterile country, a sage desert. Before him rise the snow-clad mountains, but he has weary miles to travel before he gets the real value of their benignant expenditure of clear cold water upon the vales below.

A march of twenty-six miles brings him to Crazy Woman's Fork. This river, ever flowing, is also ever muddy, having received its largest contingent of supply from the same yellow source as Powder River. Six miles northwest, and following the sweep of the Big Horn northern range, and some six to eight miles outside its general base, a new country opens. Sage brush and cactus, which for nearly two hundred miles have so largely monopolized the soil, rapidly disappear. The change is beautiful as it is sudden. One narrow divide only is crossed, and the transition is like the quick turn of the kaleidoscope, which retains indeed the outline, but supplies new combinations and new tints for every object the light illuminates.

Twenty-three miles from Crazy Woman's Fork, the bright, noisy, and transparent waters, and the rich valley of Clear Fork are reached:—so swift that mules and horses have difficulty in crossing; so clear that every fish and pebble is well defined; and so cool that ice in midsummer is no object of desire, this same Clear Fork introduces the series of natural charms that have endeared the country to the savage, and will in the future have equal beauty for those who seek homes in a new and hitherto undeveloped land.

Clear Fork is a genuine flow from the Big Horn Mountains, and is a type of many others no less constant, pure, and valuable. It is partly snow derived, and partly the sum of innumerable springs.

Rock Creek comes next, with far less pretension, but similar in character.

After passing Lake Smedt,—the great nursing haunt for ducks, wild geese, and brant, and which bears the name of Father De Smedt, who, as a Catholic priest, has ministered to the spiritual and social wants of the northwestern tribes for many years,—and only fourteen miles from Clear Fork, the traveler comes suddenly upon the two Piney Forks of Clear Fork of Powder River.

Here exhaustless supplies of pine and all affiliated trees gather about the mountain sides and crawl down even to the islands of the larger Fork, where access is easy and convenient; while the abundant game, the local supremacy of the situation and its relations to the predominating lodge trails of the country, have made this immediate region the theater of active Indian hostilities from the time of its first occupation.

Peno Creek, Goose Creek, Tongue River, Rotten Grass Creek, Little Big Horn, and Big Horn Rivers succeed, each with bright tributaries; and so, stream succeeds stream as far as the great mountain gates through which the traveler enters the rich Gallatin Valley and finds himself in Montana proper.

Nearly parallel, but distant from twelve to twenty-five miles northward from the Big Horn range, are *Mauvais Terres*, or "Bad Lands," whose conical hills and irregular outlines present all the desolate features of old volcanic *debris;* and when seen from some commanding point, appear to be hopelessly barren of good, either to man or beast.

And yet, all the rivers above named, and many others, boldly cut their way through these obstructions, and gather upon their borders rich fringes of vegetation and many elements of future development and profit.

The valleys of these streams greatly vary in width and scope; that of the Big Horn ranging from fifteen to twenty miles, and that of Tongue River covering nearly twice that area after it receives the contributions of Goose Creek and its other mountain feeders.

The region of country embraced within this outline, including the Upper Yellowstone and all east of Black Foot and Clark Passes, grasps more area of land than most of the large States or Territories; and with all its natural connections with Montana and Dakota, possesses an individual *status* that must eventually give it independence of each.

CHAPTER III.

THE NATURAL HISTORY AND CLIMATE OF ABSARAKA.

THE agricultural features of Absaraka have had incidental notice, but not sufficiently to advise a stranger of their real merit.

Wild wheat and oats abound in all the main valleys: both are grateful to stock, and sustain them well. The grasses are very heavy, so that in the summer of 1866 they were almost too resistant for easy use of machinery, and so thick that a horse could not be trotted rapidly in the bottom lands of Goose Creek and Tongue River.

Grasshoppers now and then made a visit, coming in clouds, like the drifting smoke of a prairie fire; but *they* failed to destroy the great grass region. Still they are no insignificant enemy, and a literal statement of their dense masses, put in the most guarded manner, would seem like the tale of a Munchausen or Gulliver. They cover a blade of grass until it bends to the earth. They cover horse and rider, ruthlessly dashing at every exposed part of the face or breast. They pass over with a rush, like the night roar of the cascades of the Pineys; and they shield the eye so that you can look the sun in the face as though a light flirt of snow had crossed its disk. And yet they are so subject to the mastery of the mountain winds, whose currents are as constant as they are fickle, that they quickly change their place of labor and again renew it in other fields of freshness and beauty.

The soil of the valleys is, in the main, a rich, deep loam, well adapted for vegetables, and in that climate for cereals; but alternate late and early frosts seem combined to refuse to *corn* a fair chance with other grain, while on the other hand barley, so grateful to mules, could seek no better region for its best development.

While rain, other than the dripping skirts of some mountain shower, is rare as diamonds, the numberless dashing streams, tributary to the great flows, present such ready means of irrigation that small labor and expense would apply them to all desired uses. Besides this, the deep snows of the winter season long leave the effects of their fertilizing agency, and when the autumn has turned all general vegetation from green to brown, the side hills will still be spotted with verdant places, where the lingering snow had last struggled, as if to contend with the summer's sun, for mastery of the grass it had gifted with such precocious life and protracted vigor.

Of wild *fruit* there is great variety. Raspberries, strawberries, gooseberries, red currants, plums, cherries, and rock grapes are among the number. The cottonwood-trees are often festooned with the vine of the hop, which here gives forth its product in such profusion and perfection, as will find no rival in the cultivated acres of Eastern New York.

The pine and hemlock, the spruce and balsam, the cottonwood and ash, and willow are some of the trees which are ready of access and ample in supply for the demands of generations.

The climate is invigorating and healthful. *There is no dew;* and sickness is so rare, that for days in succession, during the constant labor and exposure of 1866, no soldiers attended the stated daily *sick* call, and the hospital itself was monopolized by cases of surgery only.

The summer temperature rarely exceeds ninety, and the nights are always cool and refreshing. Few take cold; and from July 15th, 1866, to January 15th, 1867, the barometer changed from fair, or very dry, only at the advent of winds sweeping from the snow mountains, and at one storm of mixed rain and snow, near the date of the autumnal equinox.

The field of natural history is rich beyond all precedent. The vicinity of Piney Forks and Tongue River is in the very heart of the game country. It is, as between several tribes, a semi-neutral and general hunting-ground. It is a great thoroughfare for migration to and from the Arkansas, and the hills in front and rear of

Fort Philip Kearney are seamed and scarred by countless trails, where the Indian poneys have dragged lodge poles in their periodical or other changes of habitation and hunting.

The antipathy of the Indian to its occupation by the white man is very intense and bitter. The rattle of the mower, the whistle of the steam saw-mill, the felling of timber, the quick rise of stockade and substantial warehouses and quarters, are such sure signs of permanent possession, that they lose no opportunity to steal or kill when they can do so with comparative impunity. Yet the game still clings to its favorite haunts, and the Indian must press upon the steps of the white man or lose all hope of future independence. Herds of elk proudly stand with erect antlers, as if charmed by the morning music of garrison guard parade, or as if curious to understand this strange inroad upon their long secluded parks of pleasure. The mountain sheep look down from the beetling crags that skirt the perpendicular northern face of the Big Horn Mountains, and yield to no rival their claims to excellence for food. The black and white tail deer and the antelope are ever present; while the hare and the rabbit, the sage hen and prairie chicken, are nearly trodden down before they yield to the intrusion of the stranger. Brant, wild geese and ducks multiply and people the waters of Lake Smedt, and are found in nearly the same profusion all along the streams under the Big Horn Mountains; while the grizzly and cinnamon bear, not unseldom, give up their lives and their rich material for the table, when, in the pursuit of wild plums and other fruit, they are crossed by the hunter and are dropped by his rifle. Last, and largest, and numberless, the buffalo, with tens of thousands in a herd, sweep back and forth, filling the valleys as far as the eye can reach, and adding their weight and numbers to the other substantial claims of the red man to entitle this same Absaraka, "THEIR LAST AND BEST HUNTING-GROUNDS."

The Big Horn River and its branches, as well as the streams beyond, are plentifully supplied with trout, the mountain pike, and other valuable fish, and thus complete the complement of supplies with which the country is so generously provided.

Innumerable wolves do indeed pierce the night air with their howls; but like the beaver, whose dams incumber all the smaller streams, and the otter, they are forced to yield their winter covering for those nice coats and caps, those mits and blankets and leggings, which make men glad when *zero* is often reached, or the mercury calmly congeals in the bulb.

And yet, with the intervals of extreme cold and protracted snow, there is comparatively little suffering, unless from scurvy, when antiscorbutics are scarce, or men are careless, and rheumatism attends peculiar exposure. The dry snows, when in real earnest, penetrate every crevice, and drift about every obstruction. Valleys and gulches are filled, and travel is tedious or in abeyance; but the winter has its pleasures no less than the summer, and but for the hostility of the red man, the upper garrisons of that line would hardly exchange their posts for any other on the frontier.

The *mineral* field imparts some of its peculiar contributions to the stores of Absaraka. Gold color is given in nearly all the streams, as already once indicated. Whether the sources of those streams will ever equal Montana precedents, must remain for the hard labor or good chance of the adventurer, or the skill and patience of some enterprising *savant*, to determine. The Black Hills, east of Fort Reno, have indications that promise rich returns of labor, and the Lower Powder River has been left unoccupied by miners only because of the hostility of Buffalo Tongue and other Indians who infest its valley. The few excursions of a geological and scientific character, made in 1866, were almost always restricted in range and results by the exposure involved, and the absolute impossibility of procuring escort from small and hard worked commands. Small samples of lead and silver were found, but these and gold will have to be worked for. *Neither* will *often* be stumbled upon by treasure seekers; neither will they roll their offerings to the feet of *idlers* to solicit the appropriation of their pounds and ounces.

Coal is exhaustless. It can be found all along the route from Powder River to the Upper Yellowstone, and the red buttes which dot the country for miles northward are grand repositories of the same article. Lignite and the lower grades of wood coal are the prevailing type; but a vein was opened close to Fort Philip Kearney, soon after its establishment, in 1866, which was advantageously used in welding of iron, and will prove no less valuable for winter fires.

Limestone is attainable from the mountain, although somewhat difficult of transportation at present. Clay is abundant, and of such quality as to make a firm plaster coating upon simple exposure to the sun.

While the discoloration of the red buttes has been traced to the presence of iron, and it is also found in many of the sands, no ores have yet been exposed, nor have indications been made of its presence in any available supply. All other building materials are plentiful, and the tall pines furnish clear lumber of any required length or breadth, without a knot or blemish to mar their uniformity or beauty. Where some Indian fire has spread and struck a forest, so as to benumb its growth, the house builder finds his sound dry timber, which readily takes the plane and a handsome finish, and the perfection of its seasoning in that dry atmosphere is a work of short duration.

The magnetic variation at Fort Phil Kearney is 19° 20′, and its altitude over six thousand feet above the level of the sea; while half as high again above it rises Cloud Peak, completing the landscape and crowning all with its purity and beauty.

CHAPTER IV.

ORGANIZATION OF THE EXPEDITION TO ABSARAKA.

FORT KEARNEY, Nebraska, was the rendezvous where the first expedition was organized for the permanent occupation of Absaraka. With little positive information of the country to be occupied, we had the assurance that it was a precious region to the Indian; the most direct route for emigration to Montana; and then, there was the pressure of public opinion at the West in favor of the early establishment of the route, under the sanction of military authority, and its corresponding guarantees of troops and the support of connected posts.

Maps were consulted in vain for something definite in the way of description, and everybody's book which said anything about the Indian of the Rocky Mountains was eagerly read and carefully digested, from the adventures of Lewis and Clarke to the last newspaper correspondent from the Plains.

Then we had the foreshadowings of the long-heralded Laramie council to be held in May, when all the Indians of the disputed region were to assemble, and where, after the inevitable smoking and talking, a solemn peace was to be established and ratified, and a genuine right of way was to be secured to the modern land of Ophir.

Then began preparations for the march. Reports were conflicting as to whether the climate belonged truly to the frigid or temperate zone; whether the land was prolific in vegetation, or barren and worthless.

A winter's march from Fort Leavenworth to Fort Kearney in 1865, when the mercury was twelve degrees below zero and two feet of snow was first to be shoveled aside before a tent could be pitched—when the prairie winds penetrated every garment, and drifting snows often blinded any advance—was deemed a sufficient experience to decide the ladies to undertake the journey and risk the issues of a Rocky Mountain winter

It was a little drawback to the perfection of

plans for housekeeping that the only post on a line of more than seven hundred miles was to be abandoned, and that all the posts in the new command were to be built far from civilization and supplies, and in time for winter use; but seeming banishment did not discourage, after the purpose was settled to go on.

The general plan had been outlined by General Pope, who had large experience in Indian affairs, and had in view the exact relations of the new route to advancing emigration, the quickest communication with Montana, and the probability of a peaceful occupation through the agency of the Laramie council.

Northwest of Fort Laramie, one hundred and sixty-seven miles distant, was Fort Reno, formerly Fort Connor, named after General Connor, who marched to Tongue River in 1865, and returned safely, after meeting ample opposition to discourage a farther advance. This was to be moved about forty miles west, to be rebuilt for a four-company post, and two additional forts were to be constructed—one on or near the Big Horn River, and the second on or near the Upper Yellowstone. To this duty the 2d Battalion of the 18th U. S. Infantry had been assigned, under the command of Colonel Carrington of that regiment, who was also designated as District Commander, with headquarters at the *new* Fort Reno. The battalion numbered at that time just about two hundred and twenty men, many of whom were veterans having less than a year to serve, but, with the band and clerks, making an aggregate of nearly two hundred and sixty who were preparing for the trip.

General Dodge, who then commanded the United States forces in Kansas and the territories, and whose map is the only intelligible map of that country, actively interested himself in the expected movement, and within a week after he received application for a steam saw-mill, had purchased and started it on its journey. The Interior Department furnished maps. The Smithsonian gave *its* contributions. Professors Silliman and Dana, of Yale College, supplied standard English and American works upon the various departments of natural science; while *transit*, *level*, and other instruments for surveys, observations, and such other duty as would aid in the exploration and development of a new country, were also provided.

A strange medley was that outfit, and its catalogue, to which something was constantly added, opened our eyes to a clearer view of the fact that we were to live a pioneer life, and begin a new career at the very foundation of border experience.

Tools of all kinds were of course to be gathered together. Thus, there were mowing machines, and shingle and brick machines, doors, sash, glass, nails, locks, and every conceivable article that can enter into house-building. Future blacksmiths, wheelwrights, painters, harness-makers, and carpenters, who were to be hunted up out of the command, had to be provided with the implements of their craft. All contingencies had to be anticipated, so that the day of arrival in the new country should be the day of commencement, and there should then be no delay to wait for anything from the United States.

Meanwhile, the Laramie contributors to the public press were swelling the numbers of the Indians who already were or soon would be at the conference, some estimating the number as high as twenty and even thirty thousand. Certainly there were indications that the Indians were really intending to visit that post and deliberate upon surrender of the coveted route.

The death of the young daughter of "Spotted Tail," and her burial at Laramie with religious rites and many complimentary services, had brought that chief into closer relations of friendship, and messengers had been sent far and wide to bid Cheyennes and Arrapahoes, as well as Sioux, to the grave discussion.

The contingency that the Indians who occupied the territory in question might stay away, and then fight the expedition, was so remote in the assurance of a treaty, that it was hardly considered, except that it induced a request for a short delay, until the arrival of recruits who were already enlisted and on the way from New York.

The band donned additional equipments, and drilled with the Spencer carbine, and these same arms afterward proved of infinite value; while the afternoon and evening music of the band lightened the labor and sweetened the privations of our partial exile.

While still waiting for recruits, General Sherman visited the post, entering into the spirit and plans of the expedition with his usual energy and skill. At his suggestion some of the ladies began their daily journal of events, and thus laid the basis for the conversion of *one* into this narrative for the eyes of friends who could not share the trip.

On the 13th of May the recruits arrived, and were distributed among the companies to *learn to be soldiers*. With them came the 3d Battalion, Company F of the 1st Battalion, and recruits for the whole regiment, thus swelling the marching command to nearly two thousand men. But the routes to Salt Lake City were to be guarded, both the direct mail line and the northern road by Forts Laramie and Caspar, so that the eight companies of the 2d Battalion remained as the fixed detail for the Mountain District.

There was no cavalry, but as the outgoing volunteer regiments were to leave their horses at Laramie, and we were to have two hundred to mount infantry until cavalry could be furnished, the interesting experiment of determining how many could ride a horse was initiated. Fortunately, two volunteer cavalry regiments passed by, on the way home for muster-out, and the two hundred horses were procured at once. This was doubly agreeable to officers and men, as it transpired that, on arrival at Laramie, the volunteers had preferred to ride to the Missouri River on horseback rather than to *walk*, and there were not horses enough to replace a few that died on the road. As memory reverts back, it now seems fortunate in another aspect, as otherwise there would have been no horses for couriers or pickets, and the expedition might have experienced even more difficulties than it did encounter in communicating with the United States and the positions occupied. So cavalry was *improvised*. Men got upon the horses, and the majority actually made the first trip to water without being dismounted. Some men were embarrassed when the long Springfield rifle was put on the horse with them, but both man and horse soon learned how it was to be done.

At length all things were declared ready. Rocking chairs and sewing chairs, churns and washing machines, with a bountiful supply of canned fruits, were duly stored inside or outside of army wagons; while turkeys and chickens, and one brace of swine, added a specially domestic cast to some of the establishments prepared for the journey. Thanks to a defective flue, which set fire to our house, burning it, with all the contents of the attic, a few days before we left— some *best chairs*, bedsteads, and mattresses (all properly packed), with a half hundred beef tongues, some potatoes and selected groceries, were prematurely consumed; but as this was only an incident very possible in army life, the fun of the affair made up for its losses.

The last thing done looked a little warlike: the magazine was opened and all the ammunition that could be spared from the fort was drawn out and loaded in wagons; but its comparatively meager supply gave little annoyance, as Laramie would be expected to furnish the deficit in case any further fighting material should be required in the way of powder and lead. Then we had the news that a battalion of the 13th Infantry had been ordered to build a new post at the foot of the Northern Black Hills, while two companies were to keep open the road thence to Fort Reno, thus giving fair assurance that the Indians of that location and Powder River valley would be watched and held to their own theater of action in case the Laramie council should fail to establish a peace on the Plains.

The expedition had the following organization: District Commander, Colonel H. B. Carrington, 18th U. S. Infantry; Assistant Adjutant-

General, Brevt. Captain Frederick Phisterer, Adjutant 18th U. S. Infantry; Chief Quartermaster, Lieutenant Frederick H. Brown, Quartermaster 18th U. S. Infantry; Chief Surgeon, Brevt. Major S. M. Horton, Assistant Surgeon U. S. A.; Acting Assistant Surgeons, Dr. H. M. Matthews, Dr. B. N. McCleary, and Dr. H. Baalan; Battalion Commander, Brevt. Major H. Haymond, 2d Battalion; Mounted Infantry, Captain T. Ten Eyck, 18th U. S. Infantry; Battalion Adjutant, Brevt. Captain Wm. H. Bisbee, 2d Battalion. The additional officers were Captain and Brevt. Lieutenant Colonel N. C. Kinney, Captain J. L. Proctor, Captain T. B. Burrows, Lieutenant J. J. Adair, Lieutenant Thaddeus P. Kirtland, Lieutenant Isaac D'Isay.

As chief guide, Major James Bridger had been selected, assisted by H. Williams, who had been a guide to several expeditions to the Republican during the winter of 1865–6; and thus organized, the command was ready.

CHAPTER V.

FROM FORT KEARNEY TO CROSSING OF UNION PACIFIC RAILROAD—INCIDENTS OF THE PLATTE RIVER TRAVEL—REUNION OF THE OFFICERS OF THE EIGHTEENTH INFANTRY—CROSSING THE RIDICULOUS PLATTE.

FEW days on the plains are more bright and promising, notwithstanding such a cloud of dust as the plains only can supply, than was the nineteenth day of May, A.D. 1866.

Two hundred and twenty-six mule-teams, besides ambulances, were the outfit, and the band of over thirty pieces regaled us with just the right music, until the column passed Kearney City, popularly known to travelers as "Dobey (Adobe) Town."

The march was along the Platte River, whose quicksands and fickle currents have been the bane of travelers since Lewis and Clarke abused it and Colonel Bonneville crossed it. Alkaline and muddy,—sometimes disappearing under the sandy bed, so that a footman can cross from shore to shore without seeing water, and again flowing even with its banks; sometimes surfeiting the south channel, under the pressure of a strong north wind, and again, within the same sun, rolling back so as to foil the calculations of some traveler who crossed in the morning, expecting an equally safe crossing at night,— it has no disputant to oppose its claim to be the most unaccountably contrary and ridiculous river the world ever saw.

But in our course along the Platte in 1866, we had, such as it was, all the water we wished. One day was much like another day, with the same march at the earliest dawn, the same adventures with rattlesnakes, the same pursuit of wild flowers, the same inopportune thunder-storms, the same routine of guard mounting at sunset, the same evening music from the band, and the same sound slumber. Recurring Sabbaths gave us our only intervals of rest; and the fact that at Fort Reno we overtook trains which started before us, but marched *daily*, is a substantial testimony, concurrent with all intelligent experience, that the observance of the Lord's day is indispensable alike to man and beast. On such occasions Lieutenants Adair, Kirtland, and D'Isay, occasionally joined by Mr. Phisterer, tenor, helped to make something like true melody from the sweet Sabbath Bell sent us by the Sabbath school of Rev. Mr. Dimmick, of Omaha, before our departure from Kearney.

Fort McPherson, then consisting of shabby log-cabins, but now a beautiful and well-built post, was passed on the 24th of May, the only halt being to seek additional ammunition and take along an idle saw-mill not needed at that post. On the 29th we camped near the Old California Crossing, and received a call from Col. Otis and some gentlemen of the Peace Commission, who, with agreeable presents for the red men, were on their way to the Laramie council. About dark the news was brought that nearly three hundred Indians had crossed the Platte near by for a hunt on the Republican, having permission to be absent from Laramie until other bands came in and the commission should formally assemble.

"Old Little Dog," whose son burned Julesburg in 1864, came into camp and made complaint that some one of our soldiers had entered his lodge and stolen his rifle. After a somewhat curious observation of the performance of the band and special admiration of the bell-chimes, and upon being assured that his gun should be found and returned to him, he sprang upon the bare back of his pony with all the elasticity of youth and *more* than the skill of our mounted infantry, and galloped swiftly away. He had the appearance of being very old, but his agility and address in his intercourse with that pony were decidedly suggestive of the probable skill and activity of the young warriors of his nation.

Fort Sedgwick, near the so-called city of Julesburg, was reached on the 30th of May. This city, though burned by Little Dog, had been rebuilt, so as to number nearly a dozen houses and stores, and a year later, in 1867, another Julesburg, of canvas and portable frame buildings, dwellings, shops, hotels, refectories, and *recreatories*, had sprung up on the north side of the river, as an accompaniment to the progress of the Union Pacific Railroad, boasting its three thousand inhabitants, all of them determined to remain there until they could do as well or better elsewhere farther on. The water and soil of the new location were not equal to those of the Wabash, Scioto, or Connecticut River valleys: but, on the other hand, in neither of these old-fashion regions could a wall tent rent at one hundred dollars per day; neither could a piece of canvas, sufficiently large to cover a billiard table, command its thousand dollars per week.

But in 1866 we stopped three days, out of respect for the Platte. This delay was somewhat relieved by shopping calls upon the post sutler, Mr. Adams, nephew of Mr. Stanton, Secretary of War, while the troops were drawing supplies or caulking and fitting out a large flatboat, which, procured from Denver, was at the fort, nearly half a mile from the element for which its inventor had designed it.

After caulking, this apparatus had to be conveyed to the water; a double cable had to be sprung across the river, and science was summoned to do its best to adapt its heavy draught to the quicksands, shoals, and currents of the ubiquitous Platte. Two hundred men made quick work, and when the science of the learned was appalled at the magnitude of the undertaking, the common sense and practical skill of Captain Ten Eyck, an old surveyor and lumberman, solved all problems and crossed the craft safely. Twenty yoke of cattle drew the first cable over, when mules struggled in vain to start it; and Mrs. Lieutenant Bisbee and Jean were the first family passengers after the ferry was actually established. But the natural contrariness of the Platte, although so signally rebuked by the passage of a *real* boat, and permitting its current to aid in its flight, was never more conspicuously developed than when it really seemed to understand that the object of that boat was to get wagons, teams, and stores to the north bank in safety, and thereby circumvent its ugly temper. Although the river had been examined for miles to see if there was not some available ford, before shipcraft and navigation were resorted to, no sooner did that boat attempt its mission in real earnest with prospect of success than this identical Platte River fell more than a foot. Then could be seen navigation under difficulties. New eddies, spiteful currents, and outcropping bars, with desperate quicksands and the constantly varying depth of water, in turn caught it, and stopped it, and turned it, until the gallant crew actually leaped overboard. Then, partly kept out of the river bottom by a grasp upon the gunwale, and partly kept in progress by hand-over-hand along the cable, those intrepid mariners crossed that boat once again in less than four hours by the watch.

The prospect of spending until the autumn fall of water in completing the transit, aroused a fresh spirit of enterprise and developed new expedients. The slight fall of water had been carefully gauged, and, unknown to the water sprite who was plainly in league with the Sioux of *Absaraka*, and therefore opposed to our further advance, a great array of timber was procured; wagons were unloaded; false beds or frames were prepared; half loads replaced full loads, and a bold push was made to defy all elements of evil. To be sure, the lead mules would be swimming, the middle team pulling, the wheel team floundering, and the wagon would be rolling in quicksand; but the expedient of double teams always left some one or more span on the earth's surface, to pull on or push on the others. It was crossing the Platte in more ways than one; for we did it in very spite of that natural forlornness of disposition which so undeniably approximates the natural depravity of man. Enough to say that the Platte was crossed. A few mules got their ears under water, to drown from innate stubbornness. A few harness were cut to save others. Some riders had to tow the lead team with ropes; and enough whipping was applied for a week of ordinary travel. Water *would* melt sugar and cake the flour, and now and then a stray knapsack or haversack floated down the current; *but, the Platte was crossed!*

Before the consummation of this achievement, which the innovations of the railroad will prevent us from renewing, there was a social entertainment in camp not to be forgotten.

It was the last reunion of the officers of the 18th Infantry. The bill before Congress proposing to add two companies to each battalion, and thus make of each a new regiment, was already *fait accomplit;* and a regiment that alone had filled its twenty-four companies within a year after its organization in 1861, and which had received into its ranks over five thousand men, was finally to separate and prepare for new relations and new titles.

The young officers, full of regrets, but as full of life and devotion to the general comfort as ever, arranged a farewell concert of "Iron-clad Minstrels," under the supervision of Majors Van Voast and Burt. Hospital tents were unloaded and united in one grand pavilion. Camp stools and chairs from baggage wagons, or the fort, were brought into requisition, and a grand concert was the result.

It is an old army fashion to enliven the monotony of frontier life by extemporized opera, charades, readings, and the miniature drama;

and the illustrations on this occasion were excellent. The string band gave us a splendid orchestra, and the violins and violoncello, the clarionets and the flute, the French horns and the trumpet, the trombone and the tuba, alternately supplied the solo, or replenished the chorus, as the bones and banjo called for their interference. Faces only were unfamiliar; and the fifteen or twenty sergeants and soldiers, who, with fine voices, perfect harmony, and the usual *bon-mots* of Ethiopian minstrelsy, entertained the lovers of, now and then, a little sport, did as full justice to their music as they had effectually transformed themselves from Caucasian to African by the pervasive laws of burnt cork.

Then came the parting at the colonel's tent. A part of the command were to march two days longer with headquarters, while others were to leave the next morning for other fields of duty.

Captain Neil, Mrs. Neil, and Miss Bella had already occupied post headquarters at Fort Sedgwick. Captain Kellogg, Mrs. Kellogg, and little Harry, who, with Harry and Jimmy Carrington, had raced poneys daily on the march from Kearney, were also detached with Lieutenant Wilcox and two companies, and practical separation began.

Army life alone has these peculiar separations. Bound closely in social intimacies, separated from the affinities of active life in the States, the fleeting friendships of garrison or camp life are full of fraternal endearments, both in sickness and health, that go very far, when gentlemen *are* gentlemen and ladies *are* ladies, to atone for banishment and public service far from the courtesies and amenities of civil life. Hence, when tender relations *are* established and congenial spirits meet, it is painful to sunder those ties. *Then* the *esprit de corps* of families becomes hardly less sacred than that which unites officers when the ideal of army pride is attained, and each regards the honor of another as dear as his own, and jealousies and backbitings sink to the level of their own intrinsic meanness. Exceptions only prove how essential is such a law for social life in the army, and those who violate its behests, alone are degraded and suffer. No caste of rank invades their social life, neither does the parade-ground entrench upon the parlor; yet the proprieties and courtesies of good society every-where affirm their prerogatives and give delightsomeness to the relations of all.

So pleasant was the parting at Sedgwick, even with its sadness; and long will that evening recall to the old 18th its participation on that occasion when so long a good-by was begun.

Two days of marching from Fort Sedgwick brought us to Louis' ranche at the upper crossing of Lodge Pole Creek. *Now*, the Union Pacific Railroad has passed that point, and from

Cheyenne begins its borings for the waters of the Pacific. The South Platte was left at Sedgwick. The first day's march is seventeen miles to Lodge Pole Creek, and the second is eighteen miles to Louis' ranche. Here we spent another social evening with those of the third battalion under Major Lewis, a true man and perfect soldier, whose destination was Camp Douglass, by way of Lodge Pole Creek cañon, and so on to the pleasant land of Deseret and Salt Lake City. Here also we parted with Mrs. McClintick and Mrs. Burt and their husbands, and Mrs. Burt's sister, Miss Reynolds, thus still more reducing our coterie of ladies, and still farther separating us from the associations of the march and old times at home.

CHAPTER VI.

REMINISCENCES OF RANCHING, AND OLD TIMES ON THE ROUTE FROM LEAVENWORTH TO SEDGEWICK.

UP to Louis' ranche all styles of being, and the very routes of travel have changed. This very Pacific Railroad, with its swift pulse, drives everything along, and its chief engineer, General Dodge, seems to attempt the annihilation of time and space, with the same indefatigable spirit as that with which he won the thanks of everybody at old Kearney in aiding their efficient outfit for the Plains; and Superintendent Durant is tireless as he is successful. But the change from 1865, and even from 1866, when our narrative gathers its chief contributions, is marked. *Then,* no railroad stretched its hard arms after the traveler or emigrant; and the report of its coming was like the prophecies of some madmen who think that New York City will soon travel westward, to absorb the prerogatives and location of Rocky Mountain custom and commerce.

Before this railroad began its journey, travelers from Leavenworth varied their days' marches, as few will be able to do again. There was first a rough ride to the "Nine Mile Station," with its uncomfortable stone house. Then came, in turn, the crossing of the Acheson and Pike's Peak Railroad; Kinnekuck, on the Big Grasshopper, beyond Grenada, where the "*kickapoo*" Indians were buying and begging; Big Muddy; Ash Point; Big Blue, with Simpson's capital Yankee store of notions; Rock Creek; Big Sandy; Little Blue River, with its perpetual Indian alarms and occasional depredations; Little Blue Station; Spring Creek; Pawnee Ranche; Sand Hill Station; and Valley City, or "Dog Town," only nine miles from Fort Kearney.

Valley City was then ambitious and enterprising; but, in 1867, our friend Haney was the sole resident; and Hook, the old caterer for Fort Kearney, had gone farther west to establish his fortunes in some larger field of usefulness and profit. We saw him at McPherson, in June, when on his winding way, and the papers say he is mayor or alderman in the proud city—Cheyenne.

In those days, Kearney City was a busy mart of trade, and future south side railroads will restore its business. Plattsmouth and Nebraska City sent many an outfit of loaded wagons. Ox-teams and mule-teams, and teams with horses, and horses with saddles, brought many new visitors, who lunched, bartered, and journeyed on. Here, Piper and Robinson, Brown and Linnell, Michel, Thomas, Dr. Brashure, Talbot, the veteran officer, and a host of others devoted their time to the well-being of all who lingered at their doors; but it was after Kearney was passed, that the glory of legitimate ranching began. McLean and the genial Sydenham, our Fort Kearney Postmaster; Gallagher; Pat Mallalley; Dan Smith; Gilman, a man of business, straightforward and worthy, and Coles, were a few who ministered to our comfort on the way to McPherson. Then came Fitchies, Burkes, Morrows, Bakers, Browns, Beauvais, and Valentines, all accommodating and excellent. We stop to speak of Jack Morrow, the prince of ranchemen, and the king of good fellows. *He* is a rancheman indeed! Fortune has showered her favors about his life's journey and prosperity dwelleth within his walls. Keen in business, generous, and "*hail fellow*," his career, on the *South* Platte, has become temporarily restricted; but, with his indomitable spirit, no sooner did that Union Pacific Railroad shoot by his ranche, on the northern shore, than he moved ranche and all across its quicksands and waters, and went on his usual course as if nothing new had come along. A two-story frame, one of the best on the Plains, went *down*, *over*, and *up* again, as if the genii of Aladdin's lamp had been assigned to special duty in his behalf, and Jack was himself again.

But ranchemen are westward bound. Soon, they will be known no more forever! The

Pacific will stop them on *this* continent, and further than that, the future historian must write of their struggles and their triumphs. It would be just like Jack Morrow to go to Alaska, run a ferry across Behring Straits, and open a ranche for Americans and Russians who choose that route of travel from America to Europe. A tribute to the memory of ranchmen and a record of their styles and methods on the Plains is simple justice to the history of the nineteenth century. Already they are not as they were! Nebraska, one of the latest and one of the best of new States when its development shall ripen, has entertained and profited some of their best, as well as those not so ambitious or genteel.

From Fort Leavenworth to Fort Kearney, from Kearney to McPherson, from McPherson to Sedgewick, nearly all ranches have been abandoned, or the occupants only linger for the protection of their lives and property. They have had their comforts and discomforts, and among them we met some of the best and bravest and the biggest hearted men of any race or people.

To some, who have never tarried at a ranche, it will not come amiss to introduce a few samples which our experience impressed upon the memory.

Ranches alike provide for man and beast, and are arranged for their special care and protection. A large yard is surrounded by a stockade paling, with stabling, feed troughs, and hay-ricks, with here and there loop-holes for the rifle. In places of imminent peril from Indian attacks, such as Valentine's, Baker's, or Louis's, the wall of the upper stories and every angle of house or stable has its outlets for firing upon an approaching foe. The log or adobe house, which provides for the master as well as the corral provides for his beast, is often small; but, like an eastern omnibus or street car, is unlimited in accommodations for all who seek its shelter.

Let the readers of this narrative enter with us into a few sample ranches of our actual and literal experience, for illustration of their social capacity and things as they *were*, and let them envy the life of *an officer's wife on the Plains.*

Just at dark, one bitter November afternoon in 1865, when drifting snows obscured all advance, we "*struck a ranche.*" It had but one story, was long and narrow, and was divided into three apartments, each having a front window and door. Two Acheson coaches, respectively bound east and west, with the California and Salt Lake City mails, were in front, looking as if they had stood there for six months, through accumulating snow; and yet they were only waiting for their drivers and forlorn passengers to thaw and feed, and for the stock to do the same. Room *number one*, as well as room *number two*, had a substantial *earth* floor.

The former, about ten by twelve feet square, had quite a plain plank counter, and upon shelves behind could be seen the names of Mr. DRAKE, Mr. KELLY, LOG CABIN, BOURBON, and others, equally euphonious, designed to represent certain bottled products, which for a considerable sum of money were susceptible of transfer on proper demand. Some were labeled GIN, which never saw *juniper;* some were labeled RYE, which never knew that cereal; and some were simply labeled WHISKY, which were modest high wines and water, with very little of the water,—at least, so said those gentlemen who tried experiments of analysis for scientific purposes. Nutmegs, peppermint, navy tobacco, clay pipes, salaratus, baking powder, bologna, and ready-made clothing, with rows of canned fruits, furnished a large part of the invoice of the shelves; while black snake whips, tin cups, camp kettles, and frying-pans hung in profusion overhead. This room was well patronized, and in a half frozen state we rushed for its brilliant *candlelight,* waiting for further notice of *our* future disposition. Being introduced to room *number two*, we found passengers, stage drivers and the teamsters of a passing train, apparently surfeited with supplies drawn from room number one, and huddled about a table, where two big platters of bacon and cabbage, with tin cups smoking with coffee, were being disposed of as supper. The conversation of the party (for the wife of the host had been sent to the States) related mainly to a recent Indian depredation on the Little Blue, and what each one would have done if he had been there at the eventful crisis. The language had a medley of positive terms, which in New England would be called *profane;* and the prospect ahead drove us to inquiries as to the shelter of room *number three*. But, finding that ourself and children and Mrs. Neil and daughter could not agreeably share its board floor with ten or twelve characters whose social habitudes seemed only adapted to room number *one*, we threw ourselves upon the courtesy of Adjutant Phisterer and Quartermaster Brown, who soon had the snow shoveled aside, our tents pitched, a piece of the corral carefully chopped for the camp stove, and all arrangements made for hot coffee, and a good wrapping up, either to sleep or freeze. We slept, *and* survived!

Another ranche was approached, when the storm compelled a full day's stop. The mules could not, or would not go on, and the drivers could neither see nor drive. The upsetting of our ambulance, and being borne by strong men a half mile through drifts is still painfully remembered, as well as the wonderful fact that while our head was nearly broken, our basket of eggs accomplished the upset without injury. Fortunately a ranche with its usual palisade and stabling was near. The kind lady proprietress gave us her own family room; only reserving one-half for herself, her husband, and children, by the interposition of a small suspended comfort, while ample ventilation was insured between the unchinked logs, where *no* comfort was. To our jests, and especially the whimsicalities of Quartermaster Brown, an inveterate punster, always full of good cheer, who hazarded the rather profane jest that, "in his opinion, it would be hard work for the Angel Gabriel to make his trumpet reach that country,"—the old lady replied: "Well, you are the jolliest set of folks I ever saw out here:—don't see how in mercy you can laugh, and go on so!" When Mrs. Neil asked if there were Indians about, another, with more heroism, replied that "*she* had *heard* so much about Indians, and been half scared out of her senses so many times, that she had jest about made up *her* mind that she wouldn't believe nothing more, until she was *skulped!*" Mrs. Neil, with quick discernment, took a lounge near the fireplace, while the colonel and Lieutenants Phisterer and Brown took to a shed near by: but during the night the California coach came down, and its half-frozen passengers rushed for the fire. The lounge was the first object of seizure; alas, for Mrs. Neil, who was only relieved from her discomfort, by loss of rest, and the banishment of strangers, until she was able to escape, and share with us the family room, *par excellence*, of the house. Our *bill* was four dollars each!

A third ranche had its front store-room and its kitchen. Voices of men, who were ranged on the earth, like rows of pins, disturbed sleep, and the kitchen stove nearly burned our blankets, while its steaming incense no less shocked our senses; but we actually slept,—everybody was good natured, and some fresh pork and new eggs for breakfast, with a cup of our own coffee, sent us on our way rejoicing.

Louis' ranche, near the present Sydney Station, is quite a fort, and the outhouses and stables are advanced like bastions, so that enfilading fire can be had in all directions.

Such were some of the ranches of 1865.

CHAPTER VII.

UNION PACIFIC RAILROAD TO LARAMIE—COURT-HOUSE ROCK—CHIMNEY ROCK—FORTIFICATION ROCK—SCOTT'S BLUFFS—WONDERFUL FISHING—VISIT OF STANDING ELK.

ON the sixth day of June we continued our march. The first day was a severe and trying one, and will always be disagreeable to emigrants with loaded trains until Yankee skill shall perfect what has already been begun in the search after water. The ridge or divide which is first crossed is fully twenty-eight miles to the first water or timber. On the summit there is evidence of Anglo Saxon pluck, which was evidently designed to be the accompaniment of a future central ranche. About midway between Lodge Pole Creek and Mud Springs, a well had been begun, nearly twenty feet across and two hundred feet deep, without reaching water. The road across the divide is smooth and broad; but our first trip was in the hottest part of June, with the mercury at 101° above zero, and the infantry suffered intensely. Buffalo gnats flitted wickedly about, attacking neck and ears and every other accessible or exposed part of the body, and a sirocco-like wind drove the dust in our way as if determined either to petrify or melt us.

The command halted for ten minutes every hour, and officers and men alike put handkerchiefs on the head and neck to secure all the protection possible; yet there was no alternative but to undergo and *go on*. The ambulances soon filled with the lame and sun-struck, and every vacant space in the wagons was similarly occupied. No trees relieved the dismal monotony, and every halt brought into requisition the services of our patient surgeons. The tedious day at length spent itself, and we encamped at *Mud Springs*, just in time to receive the full benefit of a thunder-storm and small tornado, which grappled sternly with our canvas, and for a time threatened to unroof as well as drown us. At Mud Springs are both wood and water, but neither are abundant. In midsummer, the dry sandy bed of the stream shows only here and there a few small pools; but the shovel will soon start it, and any train will find a full supply by patient labor for an hour. It is always possible to procure buffalo chips enough to boil coffee and supply fuel for a camp oven, so that scarcity of timber in the immediate vicinity of water is not a serious embarrassment until snows cover the ground. Most trains wisely take some wood from camp to camp, and a little more permanency to this indispensable station on the route will insure supplies for sale to trains. A few log-cabins that have been the quarters of a mail guard and relay of mules, with a sergeant's party in charge, duly represent the dignity of the United States; but no one will voluntarily remain longer than to secure rest from the fatigue of the long journey of the previous day.

The march of June 7th was only ten miles to Pumpkin Creek, which flows past Court-house Rock. This stream is ever flowing, and abundance of timber can be found in the cañon near by. The rock itself is mainly composed of sand, hard pan, and clay, so that it is easily chopped with the hatchet, and thus steps are made for those who have the nerve and patience to climb to its top, nearly six hundred feet above the water of the creek. A few of our party accomplished the feat, Adjutant Phisterer taking the lead. The ascent is quite easy, but peculiar. The notches receive the toes and about half the foot, and the hands grasp the gaps above to support the body and keep its gravity within the line of danger. The return trip is not so pleasant, as the heels take the place of the toes and the back rests upon the bluff itself, just as the body was inclined forward during the ascent. The view from the summit is very fine; and far off to the northwest looms up the equally singular proportions of Chimney Rock. Centuries of exposure have evidently wrought their changes upon the great face of Court-house Rock, and constant waste is now so rapidly changing its proportions that, even in 1867, it had lost some of that boldness of definition which in 1866, and for years before, had made it such a noted landmark to the traveler.

The old road and the telegraph route deflect to the right about six miles before reaching the rock: but the present route saves nearly five miles of distance and is more readily made, although somewhat more rolling and sandy.

COURT-HOUSE ROCK—FROM THE EAST.

The above sketch of Court-house Rock will preserve its outline and present character; but, like all other odd and wild things in that region, it will soon become the prey of innovation and the mastery of Time.

The mounted infantry pitched their tents in the basin of the cañon, a short distance from the beautiful grove of cottonwood that lies at the very base of the rock, and the novel scenery made an afternoon pass pleasantly.

Twelve miles farther on we find Brown's ranche on the North Platte, and five miles more brings the traveler to Chimney Rock. While substan-

CHIMNEY ROCK—FROM THE EAST.

tially the same in material as Court-house Rock, it derives its name from a singular shaft which springs from the apex of a true cone, and is nearly three hundred and eighty feet high. It stands about five hundred feet from the bluff of which it was once a portion, and close to the level at which the cone leaves the general surface of the plain there is a stratum of true limestone, six feet in depth, interspersed with fossils indicating its origin, and closely resembling that of the quarries of Central Ohio. Chimney Rock is fast gathering about it the debris of waste, and will soon lose the bold outline and marked symmetry of its present proportions. It is now much more beautiful than when Fremont visited it, and is worn to such a fine delineation that it seems that the first summer's storm or winter's blast must topple it from its base and destroy it utterly.

Fifteen miles farther on we passed Terry's ranche, opposite Fortification Rocks, and approached Scott's Bluffs. These are also of mixed clay and sand, plentifully supplied with fossils, and throw a spur across the Platte basin so as to compel the traveler to leave the river and make a long detour to the south, or to pass through the bluffs themselves. This passage is by a tortuous gorge where wagons can seldom pass each other; and at times the drifting snows or sands almost obscure the high walls and battlements that rise several hundred feet on either side. Cedar-trees climb to their very summit and crop out in every cañon; and although these seem to the unpracticed eye like little shrubs clinging to the cliffs, the enterprising visitor who climbs to their nestling-place finds them to be full-grown trees of large diameter and proportionate height.

Fortification Rocks were so named in 1866; and at sunset the terraces and bastions, the pinnacles and turrets are quite a good embodiment of one's natural idea of old-time fortifications on a grand and comprehensive scale.

Almost immediately after leaving the Bluffs, and at the foot of the descent, after the gorge is passed, we find Fort Mitchell. This is a sub-post of Laramie of peculiar style and compactness. The walls of the quarters are also the outlines of the fort itself, and the four sides of the rectangle are respectively the quarters of officers, soldiers, and horses, and the warehouse of supplies. Windows open into the little court or parade-ground; and bed-rooms, as well as all other apartments, are loop-holed for defense.

June 12th. We marched twenty-one miles to Cold Spring or Cold Creek, which is a beautiful stream, thirty feet wide, emptying into the south channel of the North Platte.

As the Ottawa and St. Lawrence, or the Missouri and Mississippi retain their distinctive characteristics for many miles after their nominal union, so when Cold Creek strikes the south arm of the North Platte, it does not mingle with its muddy current, but each occupies its own half of the swollen stream, and so runs on its race.

A novel incident, valuable to mention for the information of other travelers, occurred shortly before sunset, which resulted in a bountiful supply of fine fresh fish for all who desired them. Sergeant Barnes took up the idea that he would fish at the junction of the two streams, and actually hooked a fine mountain pike. The news soon spread, and the soldiers gathered from all directions. For want of proper tackle a seine was extemporized. Gunny sacks were sewn together, mule shoes were fastened to the bottom for dead weight, and quartermaster's hay forks were borrowed to guide the net. Then a strong party waded in neck deep, and with one end of this seine held firmly to shore, made a half circle with the remainder, bringing it all back to land. To the great amazement of spectators and actors, just where the eddies, at the meeting of the two rivers, struggled to keep by themselves, there was a fine school of pike. A few hauls soon landed over a hundred, varying in weight from one to four pounds. Their hard white meat was excellent, and made amends for the ridiculous stupidity of the fish and the simplicity of their method of capture. They evidently were unaccustomed to visits from the white man, or could not see his approach through the turbid waters of their neighbor Platte until too late for escape.

Up to this time we had invariably found sufficient grass for all stock, and the Platte was always at hand for water.

The next day the troops forded this beautiful creek about half a mile from its mouth, and after eighteen mile's march we encamped above Jules Coffee's ranche, four miles east of Laramie. Here two of our best sergeants were drowned, being carried away by the current while bathing.

Just about sunset, "Standing Elk"—a fine specimen of the Brulé Sioux, and who, in company with "Spotted Tail," "Two Strike," and "Swift Bear," again visited us at McPherson in 1867—called to pay his respects, receive a present of tobacco, and have a talk. He asked us where we were going, and was very frankly told the destination of the command. He then told us that "a treaty was being talked about at Laramie with a great many Indians, some of whom belonged in the country to which we were going; but that the fighting men of those bands had not come in, and would not; but that we would have to fight them, as they would not sell their hunting-grounds to the white men for a road." He exhibited all indications of sincere friendship, and said that he and Spotted Tail would sign the treaty and would always be "friends." His pledge, thus given for both, and renewed at Fort McPherson in June, 1867, and often afterward, was fully redeemed, and our first interview with the Indians of the

Northwest was both the assurance of the friendship of some, and the bitter animosity and opposition of many. It was proof that the careful marching, guarding of trains, and precautions against annoyance or intercourse with Indians had been judicious, and was equally suggestive of like prudence as the expedition advanced. Thus far, with the exception of Little Dog's rifle, which had been duly returned, not an Indian had suffered from injury at the hands of the command, and those who had visited the various camps had been kindly treated, and parted as friends.

CHAPTER VIII.

FORT LARAMIE COUNCIL OF 1866—ITS RESULTS FORESHADOWED—THE ABORIGINES IN THE MART OF TRADE—HOW THE INDIANS DID AND DID NOT.

FORT LARAMIE was the center of important interests to the people of the West in June, 1866, and subsequent events show how important were the negotiations then begun, and how disastrous and costly have been the consequences of that false security as to the animus and purposes of the Indians of the Northwest which pervaded the country until the beginning of the year 1867.

The Peace Commission was in session. It was

accredited from the highest sources and had in charge great interests. The proposed general peace with the Sioux, the Arrapahoes, and the Cheyennes, and their anticipated surrender of the right of way to Virginia City, by Powder Run and along the Big Horn mountains—our very route—were matters of personal interest, independent of the difficulties that would be in the way of successfully building new forts and fighting Indians with a command that was barely sufficient to do its expected work on the basis of a permanent and reliable peace.

General Cooke had closed a published circular with the emphatic and cheering assurance that "there *must* be peace," and from leaving Fort Kearney all pains had been taken to avoid collision with Indian hunting parties who were on their way to Laramie, or who were moving to and fro in anticipation of such a visit when the council was really ready.

Our trains were habitually formed in a hollow square or corral, upon reaching camping grounds, to insure the safety of stock at night, while pickets and mounted parties carefully guarded all animals on herd as soon as they were turned loose. The strictest discipline was enforced, and nothing was left undone that the energy and ambition of the officers could accomplish to instruct new recruits and prepare them for the labor and possible conflicts that the future might unfold.

No bartering with Indians was permitted under any circumstances; but all Indians who really wished an interview had the privilege of visiting headquarters, and there received kind attention and some little gifts, like tobacco or old garments, but *never* arms, powder, or whisky.

Our camp near Laramie was therefore located close enough for business, but far enough away to prevent the mingling of the troops and Indians for any purposes—thus avoiding the possibility of collisions growing out of trades in furs, beads, and other articles, in which the Indian is generally the unlucky one, and often exhibits his disappointment by becoming revengeful and wicked.

The next day, June 14th, wagons were sent to the fort for one hundred thousand rounds of rifle ammunition, and to perfect the arrangement for supplies for the upper posts to be built in the new district. Unfortunately there happened to be at the fort not a single thousand rounds for infantry arms such as are used in the army; so it was assumed that we should have a happy journey, a happy peace, and a happy future. Twenty-six wagons of additional provisions were ready, with the single drawback that drivers had to be furnished from the command; but this nice economy had the effect, practically, to put that number of soldiers *hors de combat*, in case of any trouble requiring soldiers, and thus disposed of some of the best of our men. Major Bridger told us that he had seen kegs of powder distributed to the Indians and carried away on their ponies; but this gave no concern, as there was none for *us*.

The next day came shopping, which busied our little coterie of ladies, and it certainly had claims to novelty in its associations and incidents.

The long counter of Messrs. Bullock and Ward was a scene of seeming confusion not surpassed in any popular, overcrowded store of Omaha itself. Indians, dressed and half dressed and undressed; squaws, dressed to the same degree of completeness as their noble lords; papooses, absolutely nude, slightly not nude, or wrapped in calico, buckskin, or furs, mingled with soldiers of the garrison, teamsters, emigrants, speculators, half-breeds, and interpreters. *Here*, cups of rice, sugar, coffee, or flour were being emptied into the looped-up skirts or blanket of a squaw; and *there*, some tall warrior was grimacing delightfully as he grasped and sucked his long sticks of peppermint candy. Bright shawls, red squaw cloth, brilliant calicoes, and flashing ribbons passed over the same counter with knives and tobacco, brass nails and glass beads, and that endless catalogue of articles which belong to the legitimate border traffic. The room was redolent of cheese and herring, and "*heap of smoke;*" while the *debris* of mounched crackers lying loose under foot furnished both nutriment and employment for little bits of Indians too big to ride on mamma's back, and too little to reach the good things on counter or shelves.

The "*Wash-ta-la!*" ("*very good*") mingled with "*Wan-nee-chee!*" a very significant "*no good*," whether predicated of person or thing; and the whole scene was a lovely episode, illustrating the habits of the noble red man in the mart of trade. Of course, all these Indians were thinking sharply, and many gave words to thought, so that an unsophisticated stranger might well doubt whether Bedlam or Babel were the better prototype of the tongues in use. The Cheyenne supplemented his words with active and expressive gestures, while the Sioux amply used his tongue as well as arms and fingers.

To all, however, whether white man, halfbreed, or Indian, Mr. Bullock, a Virginia gentleman of the old school, to whose hospitality and delicate courtesy we were even more indebted in 1867, gave kind and patient attention, and his clerks seemed equally ready and capable, talking Sioux, Cheyenne, or English just as each case came to hand.

Outside everything was characteristic of the existing state of affairs, not to say prophetic of the future; and literal truth, in all its details, would furnish unrivaled scenes for stereoscopic views of Indian character and characteristics.

The council chamber was of course the first object of interest to us ladies after the shopping had been completed; and while the gentlemen were busy at quartermaster and commissary details, the ladies visited *it*. Pine boards had been arranged as benches in front of one set of quarters, and over these boards were once fresh evergreens. There was a unique and perfect simplicity in the arrangement, and such considerate *abandon* of all state and ceremony that no Indian need feel that he was kept at an awful distance, or must approach the agents of the Great Father with solemn awe or grave obeisance.

Under the eaves of all buildings, by doorsteps and porches, and generally everywhere, were twos, threes, or larger groups of hungry, masticating Indians of all sizes, sexes and conditions, covered with every conceivable degree of superficial clothing or adornment, with the special element of cleanliness just as critically wanting as is usual among the Indians of the Northwest.

During a long journey we had anticipated with more or less pleasure an attendance upon some of the deliberations, and it was understood that the colonel had, without success, requested authority to remain at Laramie during the treaty, in order to become acquainted with the Indians and learn both their disposition and decision as to the new route we were to travel and occupy. But he hurried everybody up, kept his men to the camp, and our stay was cut down to the actual necessities of a marching command. Besides this, it seemed that during the little time we did stop *some* Indians had been sent for *other* Indians, and the Indians who actually held possession of the route in dispute were not on hand when they were wanted.

"The Man afraid of his Horses" and "Red Cloud" made no secret of their opposition, and the latter, with all his fighting men, withdrew from all association with the treaty-makers, and in a very few days quite decidedly developed his hate and his schemes of mischief.

There being nothing to see therefore but loafing Indians, and great work to be done in preparation for winter and securing defensive positions before the rising war-cloud should break, we were all as eager to move on as the colonel was persistent in hurrying us forward. Some of the chiefs, however, were seen by the officers, and when they knew that the command was going to the Powder River country in advance of any treaty agreement, they gave unequivocal demonstrations of their dislike. One pleasant intimation was given that "in two moons the command would not have a hoof left." Another with great impressiveness thus explained his crude ideas: "Great Father sends us presents and wants new road, but white chief goes with soldiers to *steal* road before Indian say yes or no!" Some of us called *this* good logic.

Just as the troops left, one of the commissioners came to our ambulance and advised that very little dependence should be placed upon the result of the deliberations so far as the new road was concerned, for a messenger sent out to the Indians had been whipped and sent back with contempt. This was the conviction of all of us; still the ladies kept up good heart, and as they could not well go back, concluded to go on, but agreed to limit their riding on horseback to the vicinity of the train.

On the 17th of June, though it was the Sabbath, we passed Laramie, and camped at the Nine Mile ranche, on the Platte. We bade farewell to Laramie with great composure and no regrets. Its North Platte and Laramie Rivers, its Laramie Peak, nearly sixty miles distant, and its adventitious charms as the locality of the Laramie treaty sum up all its attractions. As at elegantly built Leavenworth, so at Laramie, water is hauled from the rivers, and a respectable fire would be ignorant of water in about a minute after it began.

This post was neglected, as were all frontier stations, during the war; being occupied by changing garrisons, whose jack-knives and bayonets, so useful in their proper sphere, had pretty much used up the pine and plaster wherever those appendages were ornamental or useful; while the parade-ground was as barren and ignorant of sod as the great highway to Salt Lake City itself. General Dandy, the post quartermaster, with his good taste and skill, had, in 1866, originated a perfect plan to secure an exhaustless supply of water, at reasonable cost, and should his successor carry his plans into effect, much can be done to redeem the forlornness of the station.

Laramie has been a profitable place for traders, and not a few ranchemen and citizens have squaw wives, and a large Indian traffic; but with some exceptions, it was to us the most inhospitable and barren post on our trip. It was then a four-company post, but was reinforced during the autumn, thus giving rise to the report of General Sanborn, special Indian Commissioner, afterward published, that, "in 1866, at Fort Laramie, when all was peace, there were twelve companies of regular troops; while at Fort Philip Kearney, where all was war, only four companies were *allowed.*"

Fortunately, this garrison proved ample for the defense of Fort Laramie, and the post was still safe on our return in 1867.

CHAPTER IX.

LARAMIE TO RENO—CAMP PHISTERER CANON—LARAMIE PEAK —WILD FLORA—PUMPKIN BUTTES.

ON the 18th of June, at three o'clock A.M., the bugle call started us from "Nine Mile ranche," and we were at last directly *en route* for our new home, passing the Dry Branch of Warm Spring, Bitter Cottonwood Creek, and, after a march of sixteen miles, camped on "Little Bitter Cottonwood," where there was an ample supply of timber, water, and grass.

June 19th. After eighteen miles of advance we came to the most remarkable defile through which the Platte urges its way in its passage from the Rocky Mountains. The river, which along the line of the march from Laramie had coursed through a prairie-like bottom, here suddenly makes a short curve of half a circle to the right, then, after passing for a few hundred feet between precipitous cliffs, suddenly turns to the left by another short curve, nearly resuming the direction of its original northwestern course, and again running through the prairie as before it sought its peculiar hiding-place.

The eastern face of this gorge is perpendicular, and nearly four hundred feet in height. On either side of the entrance are conical summits, of even greater elevation, which stand like sturdy sentinels, but having many natural terraces, on which are placed long lines of cedars as true and uniform in method as if the subject of systematic arrangement. The one on the right is basaltic, and as truly significant of its volcanic origin as are the Palisades of the Hudson, or East and West Rocks, near New Haven, Connecticut; and no part of the great wall which hems in the Niagara River, below the falls, has more stern and prison-like proportions. One or two of the ladies, with Adjutant Phisterer and Dr. Horton, went around the first curve, quite within the gorge, to hunt for agates and try the effect of pistol shots, the echoes of which were startling and many times repeated. The deep, dark waters are closely pent in and shaded by these confines, so as never to enjoy the sunlight; but all of us enjoyed the sublimity and grandeur of this wonderful natural curiosity. Old Major Bridger, in his peculiarly quaint and sensible way, dropped the sentiment: "Better not go *fur*. There is *Injuns* enough lying under wolf skins, or skulking on them cliffs, I warrant! They follow ye always. They've seen ye, every day, and when ye don't see any of 'em about, is just the time to look out for their devilment." The experience of the next morning confirmed his suspicions.

As this was the last camp before the final crossing of the Platte and entrance upon the territory of the Mountain District, it was named Camp Phisterer, in honor of Adjutant Phisterer, who selected the site, and was most conspicuous in all that contributed to the pleasure or progress of the march.

CAMP PHISTERER CANON,
North Platte River, D. T.

June 20th. Nine miles of travel brought us to Bridger's Ferry. Here we learned that Indians had, on the previous morning, made a descent upon the stock of Mr. Mills, the proprietor of the Ferry ranche, although his wife was a Sioux, and, besides his half-breed children, an Indian lived with him in his employ. This Indian had promptly pursued and recovered part of the stock, which they undoubtedly supposed belonged to emigrants. This Indian said that the marauders were "Bad Faces," of Red Cloud's band, and that we would certainly have trouble if men or animals were permitted to stray from the command. Major Bridger and Mr. Brannan were of the same opinion; and both claimed, as they had at Laramie, that we were advancing directly in the face of hostilities; and Major Bridger went so far as to affirm that the presents which were made to Indians at Laramie were given to positive enemies, or to those who had no influence at all over the warlike bands of the Big Horn and Powder River country.

Our next movement was to cross the North Platte. The beef herd was forced into the deep, swift current, and compelled to swim, and as a hundred men on the south bank kept them from returning, all were safely drifted across. The train and command crossed in the ferry-boat, which ingeniously works its own way to and fro by such adjustment of cables and pulleys, and such adaptations to the current, that the round trip was made in about eleven minutes.

The march of June 22d was sixteen miles, finding wood, water, and grass in abundance.

The march of the 23d was fifteen miles, with ample supplies of all kinds at our camp on the

North Platte, near the mouth of Sage Creek. In the morning we turned northward from the

EAST VIEW OF NORTH PLATTE, 4 MILES EAST OF MOUTH OF SAGE CREEK.
The road has crossed the ridge of sand hills, reaching point nearly opposite Fort Fetterman.

Platte, passing over the red buttes and lofty sand hills and rocky ridges which rise at least five hundred feet above the valley, and these proved in a few places to be very difficult for the more heavily loaded wagons. Occasionally the windings of the river are seen far beneath, and when the road has completed its circuit, and returning descends to the river, the panorama is exceedingly beautiful.

The river can be traced backward for miles in all its course, bordered on the north by the bluffs just crossed, and on the south by the nearly level plains, which, with slight modification, extend as far west as Platte bridge, at Fort Caspar. Near this point a new fort is being erected, with the certainty that Fort Caspar will soon be abandoned or treated as an immaterial position on the route.

Just before reaching the basin, where the Fort Reno road turns northward, following Sage Creek, and the northern Mormon road passes westward toward Salt Lake City, we found an extemporized shed of boards, where Louis Gazzons (French Pete), with his Sioux wife and half-breed children, were opening their merchandise to catch travel over the new route. Here the inevitable display of canned fruits, liquors, tobacco, beads, cutlery, crackers, and cheese were modestly conspicuous, and the good-hearted trader decidedly congratulated himself that he had the first stock of goods on the route to the land of game and gold. Little did he anticipate the doom that awaited him. Mrs. Dr. Horton was the recipient of a young antelope from Louis, and for months after we were well settled at Phil Kearney, this antelope, a spotted fawn, and two colts of Captain Ten Eyck, had each evening a spirited scamper on the parade-ground, until Indians stole the ponies and the antelope poisoned himself by the substitution of fresh paint for his usual treat of sweet milk.

French Pete will be remembered as the first citizen killed during that campaign, and especially as his long course of trade and intimacy with the Indians seemed to promise, at least for himself and family, some considerable favor if not entire immunity at their hands.

June 24th. Marched fourteen miles; camped at the head of Sage Creek; found water, but used sage brush and buffalo chips for fuel. Tufts of buffalo grass were scattered between the sage brush and cactus, so that the herds found forage without any considerable departure from the camp.

June 25th. Marched fifteen miles, and camped on the South Fork of the Cheyenne, where there is plenty of grass and timber; but the great body of the water, in extremely dry weather, passes under the sand and needs slight digging to start it to the surface and secure an abundant supply. At the middle of this day's march, just at the summit of the divide, there is the best view of Laramie Peak, showing its peculiar formation, where cone after cone rises gradually until a central shoot overtops them all.

June 26th. Was enlivened by a successful attempt to open a shorter route to Wind River, avoiding Humphrey's old camp; and after a march of twenty miles we found wood, grass, and water, besides realizing a gain of over five miles in the general line of travel.

June 27th. Marched twenty-one miles, to the Dry Branch of Powder River, finding wood,

LARAMIE PEAK—FROM THE NORTH,
5900 *feet above sea level.*

grass, and water, though the grass was largely intermingled with the inevitable sage brush and cactus. Early in the morning we obtained our first view of the Big Horn Mountains, at a distance of eighty miles, and it was indeed magnificent. The sun so shone as to fall with full blaze upon the southern and southeastern sides as they rose toward Cloud Peak, which is nine thousand feet above the level of the sea, and the whole range so closely blended with the sky as to leave it in doubt whether all was not a mass of bright cloud;

while many, even with the aid of a glass, insisted that they were immense gleaming sand hills, with no snow at all. In half an hour the air itself was invigorated by the currents from the snow banks; and even at that distance shawls became necessary, the ambulance side curtains were closed, and it seemed as if a November day was to succeed the summer's morning. In front, and a little to the northeast, could be seen the four columns of Pumpkin Buttes, nearly twenty-three miles east of Fort Reno. These buttes are landmarks for the traveler from all directions, and nearly seven hundred feet high. East of them lie the Black Hills of Dakota, and the once talked of direct route from Sioux City to Reno and Virginia City, which has been referred to in connection with the pamphlet of Colonel Sawyer published by the government.

July 28th. Passed Buffalo Springs, and down the Dry Fork of Powder River, sixteen miles, and over one divide, to Fort Reno.

The road, from early morning, was in the very bed of the stream, which, but a few inches deep, was constantly crossed by the train, and being bordered by abrupt ledges of lignite, clay, and sand, is surely indicative of an abundance, if not a surfeit, of water during the thaws of spring; while, for nearly twelve miles, the traveler is hemmed in and confined to this narrow basin, subject to constant exposure and annoyance from

Indian attacks. The grass is poor, but wood and water are abundant. Many cottonwood-trees have been felled by travelers and Indians for the bark with which to feed both mules and horses; but this leaves a supply of dry wood equal to the increasing demand.

Our first view of Fort Reno was most unprepossessing; but, expecting it to be abandoned, its ugliness and barrenness did not so decidedly shock the sensibilities as if it had been gazed upon as a permanent home, or even a transient dwelling-place. We passed through more than a mile of river bottom, densely studded with large cottonwood trees, and after fording Powder River, encamped just south of the fort, glad to have accomplished more than five hundred miles of our journey with such substantial success.

Before long, some enterprising post commander will recommend the final demolition of the fort, or shrewd emigrants will avoid it, by carrying out the feasible project for a short cutoff under the Big Horn Mountains, which was partially inaugurated in 1866, and which affords abundant supplies of grass, as well as an equal amount of timber with the present location.

So we were finally at Powder River. We had known some such hot days as are never found in the Eastern or Middle States; had drank water that had small virtue beyond its name and moisture; had used sage brush and buffalo chips for variety of fuel; but, so far, were all right and even fast seeing the country. The cactus, which annoys a horse as much as it does the pedestrian, had partly compensated for its thongs and sting by the beauty of its blossoms; and the prolific sage brush had imparted odor as well as fuel, and thus regaled the sense while it heated our coffee.

The wild tulip, larkspur, sweet pea, convolvulus, and a vine, closely resembling the Mexican plant, were among the flora that were abundant, and these, with others, were duly pressed for future care and admiration. The Indian potato and wild onion were gathered constantly by the men, and both are valuable when antiscorbutics are scarce and salt pork most abundant.

The march which brought us to Reno closed up all possibility of meeting any resident traders; and indeed, with the exception of the fort itself, there was then not a resident white man between Bridger's Ferry and Bozeman City, Montana. We were about to pass the last log-cabin, and realize practically the experience of pioneers and test our own capacity for building, keeping house, and living in the land of Absaraka! Single trains of emigrants had passed through the country. Bozeman had made one trip and had succeeded admirably in the selection of his route, and our sterling friend Bridger had a head full of maps and trails and ideas, all of the utmost value to the objects of the expedition. So we stopped at Reno, to prepare for the next, and final advance!

CHAPTER X.

FORT RENO—INDIAN RAID—FORT LARAMIE TREATY TESTED—FOURTH OF JULY IN ABSARAKA—ORGANIZATION OF MOUNTAIN DISTRICT—ONWARD MOVEMENT—MORE RATTLESNAKES—MERCURY ONE HUNDRED AND THIRTEEN DEGREES ABOVE ZERO—WHAT IT DID.

FORT RENO was first located in 1865, under the name of Fort Connor.

Absolute sterility excludes all elements of vegetable beauty or production. The single redeeming feature is the fact that the river bottom for miles in either direction is abundantly supplied with timber, so that emigrants will always find the material for fuel or building; but the same old sage brush and cactus persistently monopolize the soil for miles, and Powder River itself, flowing from the south side of the Big Horn Mountains, is muddy and so strongly alkaline as to be prejudicial to both man and beast.

In June, 1866, Fort Reno was an open post, except that the warehouses and stables had a rough stockade. Officers' and men's quarters, guard-house and magazine, were on the open plain. Being nearly one hundred and forty feet above the river, the water was brought up in wagons, and no effective effort had been made to seek for better water than that of the river, although, after our second day in camp, a spring of clear water was discovered, by the enterprise of the mounted command, immediately under the bluff. Subsequently it was decided to retain the post as part of the district command. New buildings were erected, the parade was inclosed, suitable bastions and block-houses were built, and a substantial stone magazine was completed under the immediate direction of Captain Proctor.

At the date of our arrival the garrison consisted of two companies of the 5th United States Volunteers, who were simply waiting to be relieved before proceeding eastward to be mustered out of service. A company of Winnebago Indians had been at the fort, and we passed them near Laramie on the 17th of June. Many of them wished to go back with us, but there was no existing authority to employ them, and it was generally understood and distinctly affirmed by Major Bridger that some of the Sioux at Laramie expressly demanded, as a condition of their own consent to peace, that these Indians should leave the country. If this be true, it was sharp in the Sioux, for the service lost its best scouts, and no depredations had taken place about Reno while it was known that they were there. Upon the first alarm these Winnebagoes would spring to their ponies, with rifle and lariat, regardless of rations or clothing, and, with one good whoop, disappear in pursuit. Being deadly enemies of the Sioux, it is not to be wondered that the latter should wish them out of the country; but until peace could be absolutely realized, it would have been no prejudice to that line of operations, as events transpired, to have had a few soldiers who knew the Indian styles of warfare, and were up to their tricks.

Nevertheless, the Winnebagoes departed, and their substitutes were not provided. So, as we began to live in Absaraka, we began to learn contemporaneous history.

Our camp at Fort Reno was adapted to the location. The mounted infantry were at the base of the hill, for ready access to water. Brevet Major Haymond's command was on the river's bank above, just over a slight rise, but out of sight from the fort. Headquarters tents were near the flag-staff, which had been located with view to some future expansion of the post for the accommodation of twelve companies. After a night's rest, everybody seemed busy. Three emigrant trains were in the river bottom waiting for the colonel's instructions as to their advance westward; and we were quite surprised to find that the lady travelers with those trains had no fear of Indians, and did not believe there were any *bad* Indians on the route. One train captain told us ladies we never would see an Indian unless he came to beg for sugar, flour, or tobacco.

This was all very gratifying, as this captain had been many years on the Plains, and said "he couldn't be scared worth a continental."

About ten o'clock the ladies went to the sutler's store of Messrs. Smith and Leighton to do some shopping. Suddenly a breathless messenger rushed in with the cry of "*Indians,*" and said, as intelligibly as he could, that the sutlers' horses and mules were all gone. Sure enough, upon going to the door, the horses and mules were galloping up the hills across the river, while a party of Indians were following, throwing out flankers to keep the stock in the desired direction, and evidently bending their course toward the Pumpkin Buttes. No doubt they had been eager observers of our progress, just as Major Bridger said, and no less watched the emigrants. Probably they supposed the small headquarters camp, with its large corral of wagons, was that of emigrants. At all events, they crossed the river through the timber, taking advantage of a deep ravine, and struck the herd suddenly without loss to themselves, yet passing two or three of our herds, which were under guard, without venturing an attack.

At this unexpected message all became activity. The colonel was entering the door as the messenger gave the alarm. The bugle brought the mounted men to the saddle and Brevet Major Haymond and Lieutenant Adair led eighty men in pursuit. It was excessively provoking to see the coolness of those Indians as they favored their ponies in bad places and seemed to calculate exactly how long they could take things easy and when they must hurry; but they had not long to tarry, and soon were pressing their plunder at the top of their speed.

Before the return of the party the next day, they had ridden nearly seventy miles, passing along the Pumpkin Buttes, but failed to recapture any of the stolen stock. *But* they brought in an Indian pony which the Indians abandoned when closely pressed; and this same pony was loaded with favors recently procured at Laramie. Among the variety were navy tobacco, brown sugar, a cavalry stable frock, calico dress-patterns, and other articles, which from their style and condition showed that they had not long since been taken from shelves or packages.

Indeed, the opinion expressed by everybody was afterward confirmed from Laramie, and it was thus early understood that the Indians who received presents at that post had immediately violated their obligations and commenced a new career of robbery and war.

Ten days were spent at Reno in arrangements to distribute the battalion, in reloading wagons, and relieving the companies of the 5th U. S. Volunteers. The mercury rose to 113° in the shade; wagon tires began to break or fall off;

and there was no charcoal (so Mr. Brown said) for welding and putting them in order. The warehouse was full of old supplies, and these had to be invoiced and distributed, while the quantity was twice or three times a complement for all the wagons of the command.

Business was hurried, and it was decided to leave Captain Proctor and Lieutenant Kirtland with one company to guard the stores in depot until trains could be sent back for them and the fort could be dismantled.

Meanwhile the Fourth of July came in its proper annual course, and the usual salute was fired, under the charge of Major Henry Almstedt, paymaster, an old artillery officer, and a welcome visitor at all times, especially just then, when a few things more were to be bought before launching out in that wilderness, where, except Messrs. Beal and Hughes, our sutlers, there was nothing of civilization to be had.

At length, on the morning of July 9th, at 4 o'clock, the command started. Its organization was a matter of interest to us ladies, as there were but three wives of officers left after the parting at Lodge Pole Creek, and new partings were to be anticipated, to complete the constant series which began at Fort Sedgwick.

Brevet Major Haymond, with two companies, had been assigned to the post on the Upper Yellowstone; Brevet Lieutenant-Colonel Kinney, with two companies, had been assigned to the post on the Big Horn River; and Captain Ten Eyck had been given command of the post at district headquarters, new Fort Reno, to which the change of post was to be made. By a mail received before starting, we learned from the officers that the order for a battalion of the 13th U. S Infantry, to operate from Fort Reno eastward, had been countermanded, and thus we had no rivals to compete for the honors of opening, protecting, and defending the new route and territory of Absaraka. The news gave us women a little scare, which the officers did not condescend to notice; but they, no doubt, were all laboring under the infatuation that the second battalion, with its fresh recruits, could do *perfectly* what under ordinary circumstances would have required two or three regiments to accomplish.

An order was posted at the sutler's store, telling emigrants how to corral their trains, how to deal with or not deal with Indians, and how to procure authority for proceeding beyond the post; and it is a singular fact that every reported disaster to emigrant or other train during 1866 would have been avoided, had the terms of that order been reasonably complied with.

We started westward July 9th, 1866.

The twenty-six miles to Crazy Woman's Fork, in the blazing sun, was a severe trial. It was fully night before camp was well established, and the next morning revealed the fact that half of our transportation was disabled, although inspected daily and repaired according to all the means at hand.

Crazy Woman's Fork has been described in general terms. The stream, just at the crossing, makes a sharp turn, giving two separate fords, but having quite a steep ledge or bank on the east side as the traveler enters its basin, but on the west gradually rising to the summit of the divide between its waters and those of Clear Creek.

Inspection was made, timber was cut, a charcoal pit was fashioned and fired, and every available blacksmith was put at work.

One means of repair was resorted to which was supposed to be as novel as it was effective. Gunny sacks were cut in strips and thoroughly soaked in water. These strips were tacked on so nicely that when secured with the heated tires they not only withstood the summer's use, but even in the winter of 1867 some of those wagons were doing excellent service without additional repair. Of course this would only answer where tires were unbroken; neither could it be afforded that all the corn should be emptied, except as the expenditure of the journey should permit, and thus allow an accumulation of those empty.

On the morning of the 12th, the companies that were to build "New Fort Reno" marched with headquarters to select and occupy its site. The four companies destined for the more distant posts were left to perfect repairs and follow as soon as possible. Our first camp was at Clear Fork, just at noon, and its perfect beauty and completeness of natural supplies have been anticipated in the general description of this portion of Absaraka. Little episodes, of course, occurred here, as they did elsewhere. With Mrs. Horton and Mrs. Bisbee the splendid sunset was watched with real pleasure. Our camp chairs were near the tents on the banks of the creek. A chance interruption of our meditations led to the agreeable information that we were sitting just over three valuable rattlesnakes, which an orderly was kind enough to find and mangle to death. We sat no more by the brink of Clear Fork, but dreamed of rattlesnakes until the bugle sounded the reveille the next day.

On Friday the 13th we had our next indication of Indians. A few were seen upon a high hill to the left; and after passing Rock Creek, close under a commanding ridge, our attention was called to two small pieces of cracker-box planted by the roadside, on which were notes in pencil, stating that two trains had been attacked on the previous Tuesday and Friday, and that some of the stock of each had been driven off.

These were trains that were in advance of our expected arrival, but gained greater distance than they expected, through our detention at Crazy Woman's Fork.

At 11 o'clock A.M., July 13th, we had passed Lake Smedt and were in camp on Big Piney Fork, just east of the crossing of the Virginia City road, and about four miles from the Big Horn Mountains. At last, we had the prospect of finding a home, and Cloud Peak seemed to look down upon us with a cheerful face as the sunlight made his features glow and glisten.

CHAPTER XI.

RECONNOISSANCES—INDIAN MESSENGERS—WARNINGS—LOCATION OF FORT PHILIP KEARNEY—CONDUCT OF THE TROOPS, AND ITS CAUSE.

The headquarters camp of the expedition of 1866 was organized on the 13th of July of that year with special care, and greatly to the annoyance of teamsters, as the colonel had the corral formed three times until it was sufficiently compact and trim to suit him.

At 1 o'clock he was off with a small party to visit the surroundings as far back as the mountains, and seven miles westward, to determine the most eligible site for the post. A beautiful plateau had been passed just before the command halted, which seemed particularly inviting; but as Major Bridger and Mr. Brannan had both urged that the valleys of Goose Creek and Tongue River should be first visited, no decision was announced.

On the morning of July 14th, at 5. o'clock, Colonel Carrington, Adjutant Phisterer, Quartermaster Brown, Captain Ten Eyck, Guide Brannan, and Jack Stead, interpreter, with a mounted escort, left for a reconnoissance of the region of country which had such an exalted and widespread reputation as being the richest, loveliest, and grandest of all the lands of Absaraka, viz., Tongue River valley.

Brevet Captain Adair was officer of the day, and all was unusually quiet in camp until nearly 9 o'clock, when it was found that some men had deserted to seek the gold mines of Montana. A detail started in pursuit. They returned before noon with the tidings that they had been stopped by a band of Indians, were refused permission to go on, and were instructed to return at once with a message to the white chief, that he must take his soldiers out of the country.

This party had met that same traveling ranche of Louis Gazzous about seven miles out, and a young man in his employ as teamster, who had been discharged by Lieutenant Brown at Fort Reno, had been impressed by the Indians to see that their message was correctly delivered and an answer returned.

This lad brought peremptory orders for the white men to decide for peace or war, and if they wanted peace, to return at once to Powder River. They promised not to trouble the old post, but declared that they would not let soldiers go over the road which had never been given to the whites, neither would they let them stay and build forts. These Indians were reported to be Ogillalla Sioux, under Red Cloud as their principal leader, and they had been negotiating for several days with certain bands of Cheyennes, with whom Louis Gazzous was trading, to induce them to join on the war-path and obstruct the road and all travel upon it. French Pete had already traded for a great many skins, and was preparing to visit the camp to sell as many as he could to the officers and men of the command.

The absence of the colonel induced Mr. Adair to detain the messenger in the guard tent, and shortly after an Indian messenger approached, but quickly retreated when he found that he was not promptly joined by the white man sent in advance. A demand had also been made that the white chief, in company with Jack Stead, whom they knew at Laramie, and whose wife was a Cheyenne squaw, should go and visit their village and settle the question of peace or war.

Shortly after 6 o'clock in the afternoon, and after an absence of thirteen hours, the colonel's party came in, having found two brush tepahs (tepees or lodges), where there were signs of recent occupation by Indians; but as the detachment had crossed buttes and ridges nearer the mountains for the purpose of testing Major Bridger's recommendation that a new and shorter road should be opened to Tongue River valley, they met neither Cheyenne nor Sioux.

After due examination, the prisoner was sent back, in company with Jack, to invite the principal chief and some of his braves to come into camp, when the sun was overhead, after two sleeps (at noon of Monday the 17th), and promising that they should be kindly entertained and allowed to depart in safety.

Jack returned the following night and reported that the Indians, having been alarmed by the protracted absence of their messenger, had moved off to Tongue River, nearly thirty miles, under apprehensions of an attack, but he followed their trail, delivered his message, and secured their pledge to make the proposed visit.

The reconnoissance of the day had settled the location of the fort, as Tongue River valley was not only more remote from *pine* timber, too far from Powder River, and less advantageous as a position, but *its* selection would have left to the Indians the control of the trails about Piney's and Peno, and thus given them the very gate to Tongue River valley itself; while the abundance of grass, pure water, choice timber, and wild grain in the immediate vicinity of the site selected, left no necessity for those elements to be sought elsewhere.

Accordingly, early next morning, July 15th, although Sunday, the camp, which had been temporarily on the low ground where the underbrush of the creek and dense cottonwood might afford shelter to an enemy, was abandoned, and the plateau before referred to was occupied.

Very early in the morning, the colonel and Captain Ten Eyck, with the pioneer party, had staked out the dimensions of the future post, according to plans and drawings matured at old Fort Kearney in the spring; while, to secure at the very outset a handsome and permanent parade-ground, the long train of wagons was repeatedly driven about the designated rectangle, four hundred feet square, and officers, teamsters, and soldiers, alike were forbidden to cross, except by designated avenues, while a mowing machine soon cut the grass and gave the start to the present beautiful lawn of the Fort Phil Kearney Plaza.

The tents were pitched along the streets appropriate to the respective building sites of officers' and soldiers' quarters, warehouses, sutler's store, band quarters, and guard-house; while the established general and picket guards, with the artillery parked on the parade, soon imparted form, comeliness, and system to the whole.

By 12 o'clock a stranger might have supposed the camp to have been a fixture for weeks.

We had one episode while moving: Black George ran in, in great haste, to tell missis that it was snowing, *sure;* while other reports were, that the grass of Peno valley had been fired by the Indians, and the smoke was already sweeping down upon us. All proved to be a complimentary visit from grasshoppers as large as locusts, and for a time it seemed as if wagon-covers and tents were all to be eaten up in just about five minutes. In vain were turkeys and chickens let loose against the destroyers: the whole camp hummed with the rustle of their wings as they filed themselves on the blades of grass and became familiar generally. A kind wind from the mountains came along in the afternoon, and they left as suddenly as they arrived.

The scout of Friday afternoon had determined available points for ready acquisition of building timber, and, while Engineer J. B. Gregory was soon at work trying to put in shape and operation a horse-power saw-mill until the steam mills should arrive, the whole garrison was broken into details for ditching, chopping, hauling, hewing, and such other varied duty as loomed up like a vast burden, to be overcome before winter should overtake us.

Neither was the undertaking a light one, as the district headquarters would at once become a partial depot, and supplies for a whole year had been estimated for, before the command left old Kearney.

Subsequent events confirmed the wisdom of this immediate and incessant labor; for when cold weather actually developed its power there were no surplus quarters, and the eventual, constant hostilities no less demonstrated the value of the defense and the whole arrangement of the post.

Thus, Monday morning was as busy in progress as Sunday had been necessarily occupied in location and occupation of the site.

It was deemed wise also to secure something like shape and a tenable position before the expected interview with the Indians, so as to give our visitors as good an impression as possible of our purposes and determination to *remain*.

As the diagram and map furnished illustrate the plan and surroundings of Fort Philip Kearney so far as completed on the 1st of January, 1867, no further comment need be made than to say that, with all the prophecies and liabilities that the soldiers would desert for gold leads or diggings, it was found that their almost universal impulse was cheerfully to take hold of every duty and put the work through.

The fact that gold color had been found in the creek the very first day, perhaps combined with doubt as to the safety of deserting only to run the gantlet of hostile tribes, may have stimulated labor; but never did a command apply themselves more diligently to real hard work and exacting guard duty, nor did men ever exhibit more ready obedience and willing self-sacrifice, in order to carry out the plans requiring their co-operation in execution.

To be sure, there was little kicking and cuffing and cursing administered, after the theory of some, that this is the *acme* of all discipline, and that soldiers are like cattle, to be worked by the whip and the yell; and instances of *such* discipline were publicly reprimanded and corrected, but no work, however tedious, no exposure, however protracted, no order, however sudden or urgent, failed to find willing and spirited response. Obedience was unquestioning and immediate; justice was equal and certain, and it was well understood that the colonel hated the popular theory of oaths and blows, while none the less positive in the enforcement of law. Fort Philip Kearney will be a monument of the spirit and skill of companies A, C, H, and E, 2d Battalion, 18th U. S. Infantry, now the 27th Regiment; and its own soldiers need not fear that any rivals will do more or better work, or do it under more adverse circumstances than was *their* mission in the summer and fall of the year of grace 1866.

CHAPTER XII.

ARRIVAL OF INDIANS—THE CHEYENNES IN COUNCIL—BLACK HORSE, THE RABBIT THAT JUMPS, RED SLEEVE, DULL KNIFE, AND OTHERS HAVE MUCH TALK AND "HEAP OF SMOKE."

At twelve o'clock, June 16th, a few Indians appeared on the hills, and after showing a white flag and receiving assurance of welcome, about forty, including the squaws of chiefs and warriors, approached the camp and bivouacked on the level ground in front. Meanwhile, hospital tents had been arranged for this first interview with the inhabitants of Absaraka.

A table covered with the national flag was placed across one tent, chairs were placed behind and at the ends for officers of the garrison, while other seats were placed in front for visitors.

Trunks were opened, epaulettes and dress hats were overhauled, so that whatever a full dress and a little ceremony could do by way of reaching the peculiar taste of the Indian for dignity and finery, was done. The band of the 18th played without, as the principal chiefs were brought across the parade-ground to the tents and introduced to their seats by Mr. Adair. The Cheyennes came in full state, with their best varieties of costume, ornament, and arms; though there was occasionally a departure from even the Indian originality in apparel. One very tall warrior, with richly wrought moccasins and a fancy breech-cloth, had no other covering for his person than a large gay umbrella, which, as his pony galloped briskly up, had far more of the grotesque and ludicrous in its associations than it had of the warlike and fearful.

Some were bare to the waist, others had only the limbs bare. Some wore elaborate necklaces of grizzly bears' claws, shells, and continuous rings, bead-adorned moccasins, leggings, tobacco pouches, medicine bags, and knife scabbards, as well as armlets, earrings, and medals.

The larger silver medals included, one each, of the administrations and bore the medallion heads and names of Jefferson, Madison, and Jackson. These medals had evidently belonged to their fathers who had visited Washington, or had been the trophies of the field or trade.

Those who claimed pre-eminence among the land were "Black Horse," "Red Arm," "Little Moon," "Pretty Bear," "The Rabbit that Jumps," "The Wolf that Lies Down," "The

Man that Stands alone on the Ground," and "Dull Knife."

As these were the Indians who had sent the message of the 14th, or were in their company, the question of their inclination and temper was one of no little interest to all.

The formal assurance of the Laramie Peace Commission before its adjournment, that satisfactory peace had been made with the Ogillalla and Brulè Sioux, and that the Arrapahoes and Cheyennes had only to come in for their presents, inspired some hope that possibly the reception of this first band encountered, might result in substantial advantage beyond the mere range of the band itself.

As the front of the canvas was open, the ladies gathered in the headquarters tent close by, parted its folds and enjoyed a dress-circle view of the whole performance. As pipes passed and the inevitable "*how*," the rising up, and the shaking of hands were interludes between all solemn declarations, as well as the prelude to a new speech, or the approval of something good that had been said, the scene seemed just about as intelligible as a rapidly-acted pantomime would be to a perfect stranger to the stage.

The red-sandstone pipe had its frequent replenishing before a single "how" indicated that either visitor wished to make himself heard. The scene was peculiar.

In front of them all, and to the left of the table, sitting on a low seat, with elbows on his knees and chin buried in his hands, sat the noted James Bridger, whose forty-four years upon the frontier had made him as keen and suspicious of Indians as any Indian himself could be of another. The old man, already somewhat bowed by age, after long residence among the Crows as a friend and favorite chief, and having incurred the bitter hatred of the Cheyennes and Sioux alike, knew full well that *his* scalp ("Big Throat's") would be the proudest trophy they could bear to their solemn feasts; and there he sat, or crouched, as watchful as though old times had come again, and he was once more to mingle in the fight, or renew the ordeal of his many hair-breadth escapes and spirited adventures. Many stories are told of his past history, and he is charged with many of his own manufacture. He is said to have seen a diamond in the Rocky Mountains, by the light of which he traveled thirty miles one stormy night, and to have informed some inquisitive travelers that Scott's Bluffs, nearly four hundred feet high, now stand where there was a deep valley when he first visited that country. When inquired of as to these statements, he quietly intimated that there was no harm in fooling people who pumped him for information and would not even say "*thank ye.*" Once he was wealthy, and his silver operations in Colorado might have been very lucrative; but he was the victim of misplaced confidence, and was always restless when not on the plains. To us, he was invariably straightforward, truthful, and reliable. His sagacity, knowledge of woodcraft, and knowledge of the Indian was wonderful, and his heart was warm and his feelings tender wherever he confided or made a friend. An instance of this will close the sketch of one who will soon pass away, the last of the first pioneers of the Rocky Mountains.

He cannot read, but enjoys reading. He was charmed by Shakspeare; but doubted the Bible story of Samson's tying foxes by the tails, and with firebrands burning the wheat of the Philistines. At last he sent for a good copy of Shakspeare's plays, and would hear them read until midnight with unfeigned pleasure. The murder of the two princes in the Tower startled him to indignation. He desired it to be read a second and a third time. Upon positive conviction that the text was properly read to him, he burned the whole set, convinced that "Shakspeare must have had a bad heart and been as de—h mean as a Sioux, to have written such scoundrelism as that." But to return to the council.

Near Major Bridger stood Jack Stead, the interpreter. Born in England, early a runaway sailor boy, afterward a seaman upon the Peacock when it was wrecked near the mouth of Columbia River; then traversing the Rocky Mountains as one of the first messengers to report the Mormon preparations to resist the United States, and the renewal of Indian hostilities, the same year; with hair and eyes black as an Indian's, and a face nearly as tawny from hardship and exposure; a good shot, and skilled in woodcraft; with a Cheyenne wife; fond of big stories and much whisky; but a fair interpreter when mastered and held to duty; and watchful as Bridger himself to take care of his scalp,—Jack Stead was the first to break the silence and announce that Black Horse wanted to talk.

Adjutant Phisterer, called by the Indians "Roman, or Crooked Nose," acted as recorder of the council, keeping full notes of the conference; and few were the diaries or letters home that did not embody the history of our first visit from Indians, and repeat some of their expressions of purpose or desire.

Neither did the Indian advocate appear to disadvantage, as the exponent of his rights and wants. Erect and earnest, he cast off the buffalo robe that had been gathered about his shoulders and in his folded arms, and while it now hung loosely from his girdle, stepped halfway toward the table and began.

With fire in his eye, and such spirit in his gesture as if he were striking a blow for his life or the life of his nation; with cadence changeful, now rising in tone, so as to sound far and wide over the garrison, and again sinking so as to seem as if he were communing with his own spirit rather than feeling for a response from the mind of another, the Cheyenne chief stood there to represent his people, to question the plans of the white chief, and solemnly advise him of the issue that was forced upon the red man. It was an occasion when all idea of the red man as the mere wild beast to be slaughtered, quickly vanished in a prompt sympathy with his condition, and no less inspired an earnest purpose, so far as possible, to harmonize the intrusion upon his grand hunting domain with his best possible well-being in the future.

Other chiefs folowed "Black Horse," in harangues of varied length and vigor; and all agreed that they preferred to accept protection and become the friends of the whites. They came to represent one hundred and seventy-six lodges, and had been hunting on Goose Creek and Tongue River, when they met Red Cloud; but said that one hundred and twenty-five of their young men were absent with "Bob Tail," having gone to the Arkansas on the war-path and hunt. They had quarreled with another band of Cheyennes, who lived near the Black Hills east of Powder River; and said there was a third band south of the Republican hostile to the whites. Two of the chiefs had with them Camanche wives whom they had married in excursions to the south.

They gave the history of a portion of our march, and stated correctly, what Red Cloud had assured them, that half of the white soldiers were left back at Crazy Woman's Fork. They said that Red Cloud told them, the morning before the messenger was sent to the camp, that white soldiers from Laramie would be at Piney Fork before the sun was overhead in the heavens; that the white chief sent soldiers from Reno after Indians who stole horses and mules; but the white soldiers did not get them back.

They also stated that the Sioux were having a sun-dance, insisting that the Cheyennes must make common cause with them and drive the white man back to Powder River; that some of Red Cloud's men had already gone back to interrupt travel on the road; that they had left their squaws in the village with thirty of their old men, and were afraid the Sioux would rob them in their absence if they should stay too long in the white man's camp; but that if they could have provisions, they would make a strong peace, and let a hundred of their young men, whose return would be in two days, go with the white soldiers against the Sioux.

Before the council broke up, Brevet Major Haymond arrived with his four companies and went into camp northwest of the fort near the river crossing.

The Indians became very restless as the afternoon progressed, and at last bade good by; receiving papers indicative of their good behavior, and entering into an agreement to leave the line of road and go upon or south of the upper plateau of the Big Horn Mountains. They afterward visited Fort Caspar, behaving well, and no doubt observed their obligations as best they could.

The presents given consisted of some second-hand clothing of the officers, twenty pounds of tobacco, a dinner of army rations, and enough flour, bacon, sugar and coffee to give them a meal in their village and convince the absent of their kind treatment. They left with apparently cordial good feeling, and the understanding that they were not to approach emigrant trains even to beg; but might go to Laramie, or other military posts when hungry, as long as they remained the friends of the whites.

There is no evidence that any of these chiefs have violated their pledges.

CHAPTER XIII.

MASSACRE OF LOUIS GAZZOUS' PARTY—INDIAN RAID AND GREAT LOSS OF MULES—THE CHEYENNES AGAIN—FORTY HOSTILE DEMONSTRATIONS OF THE "PEACEABLE TRIBES"—THE LARAMIE TREATY INCIDENTALLY TESTED—MASSACRE OF LIEUTENANT DANIELS—A FIGHTING PARSON.

AT five o'clock A.M., July 17th, the herds of Brevet Major Haymond were surprised, the Indians crawling within the picket, and with great sagacity starting Wagonmaster Hill's bell mare first, so as to secure all in company. Major Haymond, with one orderly, started in pursuit, as we afterward learned, although no information was given at the post until two hours after. He left orders, we heard, for the mounted men to saddle and follow. The party thus pursuing in haste was ultimately surrounded by several hundred Indians, and when a messenger was sent in with report of the condition of affairs, two companies of infantry and fifty mounted men, with ammunition, rations, wagons, and ambulances, were at once started to the relief.

But very soon sad reports came from Peno valley, only a few miles over Lodge Trail Ridge. The casualties of the command had been two men killed and three wounded; and, more painful than all, was the report of the massacre on the road of Louis Gazzous and most of his party.

Brevet Major Haymond, finding the Indians so numerous and the ground impracticable for the use of his men, while the Indians were not only perfectly at home, but specially watchful of stragglers and fully versed in that style of warfare, fell back toward the post. On the retreat he came up with the wagons of French Pete, which had already started for camp. About the plundered wagons lay the mutilated remains of his party, with the exception that his wife, a Sioux woman, with her five children, had been able to hide in the brush until the arrival of the troops furnished an escort to headquarters.

Six men lay dead and mutilated upon the road. Such was the first lesson to the expedition of the kind of peace to be expected for the future. Henry Arrison, of St. Louis, partner of Gazzous, was among the number. The cattle, wagons, and goods that the Indians had not broken open, for want of time, were brought to the post and taken charge of by Mr. John W. Hugus, administrator, on behalf of the widow, creditors, and friends of the deceased.

The Sioux wife of Gazzous said that the Cheyennes had traded largely and pleasantly with Pete, and that the chiefs who had visited the post on the 16th were with them until midnight, smoking and trading; that during the evening some of the Sioux chiefs came up from Tongue River valley and asked Black Horse what the white man said to them, and whether the white chief was going back to Powder River. To this Black Horse answered "that the white chief would not go back, but his soldiers would go on." They then asked "what presents were given." Black Horse told them "that they had all they wanted to eat, and the white chief wished all the Arrapahoes and Sioux, and all other Indians of that country, to go to Laramie and sign the treaty and get their presents." At this the Sioux unstrung their bows, and whipped Black Horse and the other Cheyennes over the back and face, crying "*Coo!*" which by the Indians is deemed a matter of prowess and a feat which secures them credit, as they count their "*Coos*" in a fight almost as proudly as they do the scalps of enemies.

After the Sioux left, Black Horse told French Pete that he must go to his village and from there to the mountains, for the Sioux meant war, but advised *him* to send a messenger to the white chief quick, or the Sioux would kill him. French Pete neglected the advice; but was on his return in the morning, when the Sioux, who had stolen Major Haymond's mules, and had come in contact with his men, came across the train and destroyed all the men who were with it.

On the same day Major Haymond's four companies were ordered to change their position and encamp just below the fort.

On the 19th a train with military escort, under Captain Burrows, was sent back to Fort Reno for provisions. The young men of the Cheyennes also returned from the Arkansas, and "Bob Tail" had an interview with the colonel, leaving his own robe as a pledge of his friendship.

About one o'clock A.M., July 24th, a courier from Clear Fork brought a dispatch from Captain Burrows that the Sioux were very numerous, and additional force was needed at once. Mr. Thomas Dillon also wrote that Mr. Kirkendall's train had been engaged all the afternoon, and he could not move without troops. A company of infantry, with a mountain howitzer, was soon started, and upon their approach in the morning, the Indians, numbering several hundred, fled. Torrence Callery, of Company G, had been killed; and one of the trains relieved, which had been taken back to Fort Reno temporarily, contained five officers of the regiment, with servants, baggage, Mrs. Lieutenant Wands and child, all of whom had been forwarded from Fort Laramie, under the prestige of the Laramie treaty, with only ten men as escort to headquarters. When this train had reached Crazy Woman's Fork it was attacked by fifty Indians, and

Lieutenant Daniels, of Indiana, who was a little in advance selecting camping ground, was killed, scalped, and mutilated, while one of the Indians put on his clothes and danced within view of the party.

Chaplain David White, Lieutenants Templeton, Bradley, and Wands, with Mrs. Wands and child, survived, and the Henry rifle of Mr. Wands was specially efficacious in warding off and punishing the assailants.

Chaplain White, like the preachers of Cromwell, only prayed *internally*, while putting his time physically into the best exercise of self-defense. He thinks he did his duty; and the officers say that he thought it was just about the right thing to kill as many of the varmint as possible.

Lieutenant Kirtland's rescuing party from Reno was also very prompt, and Lieutenant Daniel's remains were escorted to that post and suitably buried.

The Cheyennes of *Black Horse* met Kirkendall's train and gave warning of the approach of the Sioux, just as they had at the council given indications of this same movement. The warning was disregarded, but the Sioux *did* come.

Thus commenced our first two weeks in our new home. A few more incidents will illustrate the experience that followed.

July 22d. At Buffalo Springs, on the Dry

Fork of Powder River, a citizen train was attacked, having one man killed and another wounded.

July 22d. Indians appeared at Fort Reno, driving off one public mule.

July 22d. Mr. Nye lost four animals near Fort Phil Kearney, and Mr. Axe and Mr. Dixon each had two mules stolen by Indians.

July 23d. A citizen train was attacked at the Dry Fork of the Cheyenne, and two men were killed.

July 23d. Louis Cheney's train was attacked; one man was killed, and horses, cattle, and private property were sacrificed.

July 28th. Indians attempted to drive off the public stock at Fort Reno, and failed; but took the cattle of citizen John B. Sloss. Pursuit; recovered them.

July 29th. A citizen train was attacked at Brown Springs, four miles east of the East Fork of the Cheyenne, and eight men were killed, two were wounded, and one of these died of his wounds. Their grave is still memorial of the confidence with which they left Laramie, assured that all was peace. These men, though too few in numbers, were well armed, but were deceived by a show of friendship; and one Indian shot a white man in the back just after shaking hands and receiving a present.

Meanwhile, the necessity of maintaining Fort

Reno as an intermediate post on the route had been established. Another company was sent to reinforce its garrison. The Upper Yellowstone post was abandoned for want of troops, and early in August, Brevet Lieutenant-Colonel N. C. Kinney, with Captain Burrows and their two companies, were sent to the Big Horn River, distant ninety-one miles, to establish that post, subsequently known as Fort C. F. Smith.

The narrative of *all* hostile demonstrations need not be traced. Enough will be given to correct false ideas as to the feelings and operations of Indians during the year; and the reader will not be astonished that ladies, as well as gentlemen, perused the President's message of December 8th, 1866, which congratulated the country that the Indians were at peace, with something like inquisitiveness as to whether the colonel had reported the true condition to department headquarters, and whether department headquarters had read his report.

But to proceed. Grover, the artist, correspondent of Frank Leslie, was scalped one Sunday morning, while only a few minutes' walk from the post.

August 9th. In one of the frequent attacks upon the timber train, four mules were taken after the driver had cut them loose; but a party from the fort under Corporal Phillip recaptured the mules, killing one Indian and wounding a second.

August 12th. Indians drove off horses and cattle belonging to citizens encamped on the river bank near Reno. The cattle were re-captured.

August 14th. Joseph Postlewaite and Stockley Williams were killed within four miles of Fort Reno.

August 17th. Indians appeared in force near the same post, and drove off seven public horses and seventeen mules. Other similar depredations occurred in August.

September 8th, at 6 o'clock A.M. Twenty mules were driven from a citizen herd, during a severe storm, within a mile of Fort Phil Kearney; and two other demonstrations were made the same day. The colonel with one party, and Lieutenant Adair with another, were out until after 9 o'clock at night in pursuit.

September 10th. Ten herders were attacked a mile south of the fort, losing thirty-three horses and seventy-eight mules. Pursuit was vigorous, but unsuccessful.

September 13th. At midnight a summons came from the hay contractors, Messrs. Crary and Carter, at Goose Creek, for help, as one man had been killed, hay had been heaped upon five mowing-machines and set on fire, and two hundred and nine cattle had been stolen by the

Indians, who had driven a herd of buffalo into the valley, and thus taken buffalo and cattle together out of reach.

Lieutenant Adair went at once with reinforcements, but found the Indians in too large force for continuance of the work.

The same day at 9 o'clock, Indians stampeded a public herd, wounding two of the herders. Captain Ten Eyck and Lieutenant Wands pursued until late at night. Private Donovan came in also with an arrow in his hip; but, just as he was always in an Indian fight, brave as a lion, started out again as soon as it was withdrawn.

September 14th. Private Gilchrist was killed.

September 16th. Peter Johnson, riding a few rods in advance of his party, which was returning from a hay field near Lake Smedt, was suddenly cut off by Indians. Search was made that night by a party under Quartermaster Brown, but his remains were not recovered.

September 17th. A large force demonstrated from the east, and took forty-eight head of cattle; but all were recaptured on pursuit.

September 20th. Indians attacked a citizen outfit lying in the angle of the two Pineys; but were repulsed by aid from the fort, losing one red man killed and another wounded.

September 23d. Indians attacked and drove off twenty-four head of cattle. They were pursued by Quartermaster Brown, in company with twenty-three soldiers and citizens, and after a sharp fight at close quarters, the cattle were recaptured, and a loss was inflicted upon the Indians of thirteen killed and many wounded.

September 23d. Lieutenant Matson, with an escort, bringing wagons from the hay field, was surrounded and corraled for some time by a superior force. He found upon the road the body of contractor Grull, who had been to Fort C. F. Smith with public stores, and was killed on his return with two of his drivers.

On the 17th, 21st, and 23d, Indians had also been active near Fort Reno, driving off horses and cattle. Casper H. Walsh was killed; and at the Dry Fork of the Cheyenne, citizens W. R. Pettis and A. G. Overholt were wounded.

September 27th. Private Patrick Smith was scalped at the Pinery, but crawled a half mile to the block-house, and survived twenty-four hours.

Two of the working party in the woods were also cut off from their comrades by nearly one hundred Indians, and were scalped before their eyes. A party of fifteen dashed at the nearest picket but did no harm.

Captain Bailey's mining party lost two of their best men.

On one occasion a messenger came in hot haste from the Pinery, reporting that they were besieged; that the Indians had fired through the loop-holes of the block-house; that the men were constantly under arms, unwilling as well as unable to work, and asking for a force to clear the Indians out of the bottom lands underneath, where the woods were very dense. The colonel went out with a small party and howitzer, shelled the woods, restored confidence, and the men resumed work. A person ignorant of the effect of a case shot, which scatters its eighty iron bullets quite dangerously, might think it very foolish to explode one where no enemy was *in sight:* but we saw those experiments repeated, where otherwise quite a skirmishing party would have been required, and as the Indians invariably ran away, and sometimes got hurt, the little howitzers were soon favorites and no objects of ridicule or contempt.

The foregoing are instances out of many Indian visits, but do not give all, even of the first two months of our residence in that country. Alarms were constant; attacks upon the trains were frequent, and this kind of visitation continued during the whole season. The ladies all came to the conclusion, no less than the officers affirmed it, that the Laramie treaty was " *Wau-nee-chee*," NO GOOD!

CHAPTER XIV.

CONDUCT OF THE CROW INDIANS—WHAT BRIDGER AND BECK-WITH SAY.

IT was quite early after the establishment of Fort Philip Kearney that measures were taken to hold communication with the Crow Indians, to consult with the authorities of Montana, and determine the condition of the entire route to Virginia City. Major Bridger was selected for the mission, accompanied by Henry Williams, assistant guide, who proved himself valuable in almost every work he undertook. They made the through trip with comparative expedition, made complete notes of the journey, and besides their official reports, were very courteous in contributing their information to those who were desirous to keep a full record of all that transpired during our sojourn on the frontier.

They had first an interview with nearly six hundred warriors, not far from Clark's Fork. On that occasion "White Mouth," "Black Foot," and "Rotten Tail" declared their uniform and unanimous voice for peace; but said that in some instances the young men desired to join the Sioux, and thus come to some accommodation as to their title to the lands of which they had been robbed by both Sioux and Cheyennes.

Red Cloud had made them a visit and they had returned the visit, but would not join him against the whites. The "Man afraid of his Horses" told them that his young men were going on the war-path, and that the Sissetons, Bad Faces, Ogillallas from the Missouri, the Minnecongous from the Black Hills, the Unkpapas, some Cheyennes and Arrapahoes, as well as the Gros Ventres of the Prairie, were united to drive away the whites, and would have big fights at the two new forts in the fall.

They also represented that "Iron Shell," with some of the young men of the Minnecongous and Brulès, would go with Red Cloud, notwithstanding the Laramie treaty; that the Nesperces and Flatheads were friendly, but the Pagans and Bloods were hostile, while the Blackfeet, Assiniboines, and Crees were friendly with both parties and would join no league against the whites.

Besides the visits of Bridger to other bands of Crows along the route from Big Horn to the Upper Yellowstone, James Beckwith, the famous mulatto of the plains, who had also lived among the Crows as an adopted chief, and had several Crow wives, was employed as an assistant guide, and was sent to their villages, where he subsequently sickened and died.

From these sources it was learned that in the

fight of September 23d the Sioux lost thirteen killed and had a great many wounded.

Other parties of Crows came to Fort C. F. Smith to hunt and trade in that vicinity, and not only showed uniform friendliness toward the whites and the new road, but offered two hundred and fifty young warriors to engage in operations against the Sioux. Major Bridger had great confidence in this proposition; but the officers had, it would seem, no authority to employ so many, as well as no means of arming and equipping them when employed.

All the statements of the Crows were substantially confirmed by Cheyennes at a subsequent visit. They represented "Red Cloud" and "The Man afraid of his Horses" to be in Tongue River valley, and "Buffalo Tongue," to be on Powder River; that the "Big Bellies," the "Bad Arrows," "Those that wear a Bone in the Nose," and "Those that put Meat in the Pot" were near the Big Horn River, and though friendly to the Crows were opposed to the road; that "Bob North," a white man with but one thumb, with twenty-five lodges and the "Big Medicine Man of the Arrapahoes," had also joined the aggressive party.

Still later in the season there was renewed and cumulative evidence that the Crows were truly friendly, but were unwilling to venture very far eastward for any purpose, until the Sioux were out of the way or the white soldiers were sufficiently numerous to guarantee their safety without sacrifice of life or property.

"White Mouth" and "Rotten Tail" told Mr. Bridger that they were half a day in riding through the hostile villages in Tongue River valley, and that fifteen hundred lodges of war parties were preparing to attack the white man at Fort Philip Kearney and Fort C. F. Smith.

All these statements were believed, and it is known that they had important influence in that vigorous prosecution of necessary work which followed, and rendered impossible any system of aggressive war on the part of the troops of the garrison

CHAPTER XV.

VISIT OF INSPECTOR-GENERAL HAZEN—REINFORCEMENTS ON THE WAY—MOUNTED INFANTRY COMPARED WITH SIOUX LIGHT CAVALRY—UNITED STATES MAILS—CORRAL SYSTEM —TIMBER AND LUMBER SUPPLIED TO ORDER.

The last days of August brought Brevet Brigadier-General Hazen on a tour of inspection, and his visit was greatly enjoyed by us all. He also brought the welcome news that two companies of regular cavalry had been ordered up immediately from Laramie, and that although he had waited a week for them at Fort Reno, they would certainly be but a few days behind him. The next day it was understood that official orders had been received to the same effect—that one regiment of infantry had left St. Louis by way of reinforcements westward, and that General Cooke had acquired the other two battalions of the 18th, with control of all operations on the Platte. This inspired everybody with good cheer, and the time was eagerly anticipated, by ladies no less than gentlemen, when adequate means would allow some opportunity to punish Indians more thoroughly and thus insure the integrity and security of the route.

On the last day of August General Hazen, accompanied by Lieutenant Bradley and twenty-six picked men of the mounted infantry, with Mr. Brannan as guide, started overland for Fort Benton and other posts on the Upper Missouri. The loss of one-third of the mounted force seemed less annoying, as the two companies of cavalry were supposed to be not far behind, and yet, in fact, they *did not come that fall.* Half armed portions of one company straggled along in November, having old Enfield rifles or old-fashion carbines, and the first installment of this company was but sixteen strong, under a sergeant, with orders to escort a train to Fort C. F. Smith. All this no one could know in advance; and the constant looking for somebody to help watch, work, and fight was kept up until, as in respect of almost everything else relating to the post which was of importance to be known to the people at large, or at least the authorities at the head of affairs, it was left for the massacre of December 21st to arouse the impression that there were really some untamed red men roaming loose on the plains.

The mounted infantry were the sole dependence for carrying the mails, as these had been ordered to be carried weekly, at the rate of at least fifty miles per day; and the horses, which by the 10th of October had been reduced to less than forty, were poorly adapted for a swift express of over two hundred and thirty-five miles without a relay, and especially when they were almost daily required for active picket and outpost duty at the fort.

This mail was our sole reliance, as it made the trip both ways, and no cavalry or other mail parties came from Laramie to exchange with it, and so divide the labor between the two posts until subsequently, when mails were left at the ferry. Fort Philip Kearney therefore did not receive its mails from the east, but sent east when it wanted some news, and thus occupied a very prominent and independent position in Absaraka and the region adjacent thereto. Sometimes these trips were as long as three weeks, because night travel had to be relied upon through a portion of the route, and neither wagon-teams nor pack mules maintained their ambition as to speed and exactness, when they found that their natural inability to perform the feat was not regarded as excuse for failure.

The Indian habit of calling as early as daylight for loose stock, required also that the horses, when in garrison, should be early saddled, so that, at any moment, the girths could be tightened, the bridles be bitted, and a dash be made after such persistent trespassers. It was a source of congratulation, alike to men and to horses, that this habit never cost the garrison a life or a horse, while in many cases it defeated the plans of the Indians and secured the recapture of stolen stock. Mounted infantry, however, are a peculiar institution in that country. The long rifle, however well cared for, is forever in the way, and the soldier is spoiled for a footman and is almost useless in the saddle. It became a settled opinion, which the ladies shared with others, that the Sioux and Cheyenne light cavalry were much better adapted to the hills and valleys, the gorges and mountain passes, especially in a long race, or steeple-chase, than even the mounted men of the 18th. Of course, it was difficult for men, unused to horseback-riding, to take to it *kindly*, at first; and the manual of arms was less convenient when yelping Indians were shaking buffalo robes and speeding the flight of arrows and bullets. We had, of course, to keep a mounted picket and prompt communication with working parties; and there was also some responsibility for helping Fort C. F. Smith to some communication with the outer world.

Such men as Brannan, with his daring, who was scalped through his imprudence on his return from the trip with General Hazen; as Van Volzpah, with his experience and quiet coolness, who, after a life in Oregon and Washington Territories, and many successful trips to Laramie, was butchered at last, with his whole party; as miner Phillips, with his sound sense and solid honesty, who carried dispatches on the night of December 21st; and Captain Bailey, of the miners, who, after seventeen years in frontier explorations, retained the manners and habits of a pleasant gentleman, full of intrinsic worth and steady courage, could do anything with Indians or horses on a mail trip, that *anybody* could do; but in that bracing climate horses *would* need their forage when trips were frequent, and even the men were found to be limited to something like the ordinary finite range of physical ability and endurance. And yet, nearly every ten days, and sometimes each week, brought us a mail, omitting such newspapers as were borrowed somewhere east, or were diverted to Salt Lake City, where there were more readers, as well as the leisure of security from the red men of the plains. New York papers were often ten weeks old, and nearly half the letters, for a portion of the time, bore the postal mark of Salt Lake City, additional to several others.

When horses diminished in numbers, and mounted escorts could not accompany the trains to the Pinery, a new plan was adopted for the more prompt formation of the corral. Trains went out in two parallel lines with an intervening space of fifty or one hundred yards, so that, when an alarm was given, the front wagons turned in to meet each other; those on the flanks were trotted up with the mules inside, covered by the next wagon in advance; while the rear wagons of each line obliqued in to fill the fourth, or rear side of the square. It was a singular commentary on the recklessness of travelers, their ignorance of the feelings of Indians, their want of correct advice at Laramie, and the wisdom of the Indians themselves,—that, of all the outrages committed on trains in 1866, there was never a single persistent attack upon a good corral, neither was there loss of life when proper rules were regarded. The apparent exception near Fort Philip Kearney, when Lieutenant Guinness was killed, in June, 1867, grew out of the great disparity of numbers, in part, and partly to the assurance of the Indians, derived from the massacre of December 21st, 1866. Brevet Major Powell, who resisted the attack of June, 1867, also resisted the tantalizing challenge of Indians, December 19th, 1866, and literally obeyed his orders, thereby saving himself and command from that utter destruction which befell others two days later.

For many months nearly all public references to attacks about that post, only made mention of attacks on *wood* trains; and the world at large seemed to regard it as if a detail had each time been sent for daily supply of fuel, instead of being employed on systematic labor in building a large post and fort.

The Pinery, which is most accessible, is just seven miles from the fort, as indicated on the map of Fort Philip Kearney and surroundings. At the base of the upper mountain, as well as on the island below, block-houses had been built, and the men for a long time remained over night for early morning work. A train of over ninety wagons was employed at one period, and the timber would be cut, loaded, and hauled the same day. All sizes were accessible, from timber that would work out thirty-inch clear boards and plank down to the slender pine of the thickets from two to three inches thick, which made a close framework or skeleton for support of a clay covering. Innumerable straight trees of from four to fifteen inches in diameter were found, which cut from thirty to forty feet in length, without a knot or branch; and these lay so closely in a wall as to need no chinking before the plaster was applied.

These timber parties always had their armed teamsters, their armed choppers, and armed guard. Chopping details varied from sixteen to thirty, with a special guard of about the same number, making, with teamsters, a resisting force of from seventy to one hundred men, and sometimes, early in the season, the force of teamsters and wagonmasters alone was nearly that number.

Timber was procured much nearer, but with more difficulty, in July and August; and the place last adopted proved ample for all purposes.

This work blended all kinds of labor appropriate for tools that chop, saw, hew, or finish *wood*. Shingles were rived from bolts sawed by the men, and many a "shingle bee" was held, at night, to expedite work and convince the skeptical that shingles, or anything else, could be made or *done*, when it *had* to be, and that civilization was still westward bound.

CHAPTER XVI.

FORT PHILIP KEARNEY AND SURROUNDINGS — A PICNIC — ASCENT OF THE MOUNTAINS — LAKE SMEDT — FINE SCENERY — PLAN OF THE FORT.

But for the presence of hostile Indians, the country about Fort Philip Kearney would be a charming field for hunting and picnic purposes. Soon after our arrival, the ladies ventured twice to the mountains, and the second time descended to Pine Island, where choice elk steaks, furnished by the timber choppers, and suitable accessories, supplied a delightful meal, and no Indian disturbed the pleasure. Judge J. T. Kinney, formerly Chief Justice of Utah, representing the business interests of Mr. Botsford, the sutler, was chief manager and steward, and under his skillful catering a dinner was provided that would not have dishonored a city restaurant.

The bill of fare was not printed; but canned lobster, cove oysters, and salmon were a very fair first course; and, associated with the game, were jellies, pineapples, tomatoes, sweet corn, peas, pickles, and such creature comforts, while puddings, pies, and domestic cake, from doughnuts and gingerbread up to plum cake and jelly cake, with coffee, and Madame Cliquot for those who wished it, and pipes and cigars for the gentlemen, enabled everybody to satisfy desire.

A trip to Lake Smedt, which is but a little more than two miles distant, is another locality which could be made a pleasant summer resort, to say nothing of skates in winter. The western end of the lake is accessible by a gentle slope after crossing Starling Creek; and a few hours' work and the use of pine timber would make a convenient landing for sail boats and duck boats. The north shore is ragged and the hills are covered with fragments of coal, red lava, and melted boulders, which seem as if they had been thrown out of some great furnace. The south shore is hilly but less rocky. The water is deep and intensely alkaline, and there is neither inlet nor outlet as the little creek which is crossed before reaching the lake passes by the west end at a few hundred yards distance, and turns westward to the Piney Forks, emptying its stream below their junction.

A third ride, which requires the saddle, is to

climb the mountains by an Indian trail just below the point where the Little Piney makes its exit, and visit Fort Ridge, more than seven hundred feet above the fort. This ridge received its name from an Indian fort near the summit. It is about thirty feet square, of loose stones of considerable size, and when visited, the inclosure was raised still higher by temporary abattis of pine logs. There were indications that a band had recently camped near it, having squaws with the party, and doubtless this place furnished one of the camp fires which had repeatedly been observed both by night and day. The view from the next higher range is fine beyond description.

Below the observer, the fort, the Pineys, Lake Smedt, and the branches of Peno Creek are drawn so near that it is difficult to realize that they are from seven to twelve miles distant. Beyond, and northward, the successive round-topped red buttes follow each other like an exaggerated style of the waves of some old cornfield which has been uncultivated for years; and thus they stretch on for nearly eighty miles before they are blended with the uneven horizon. In the northwest is the beautiful valley of Tongue River and its tributaries, with the Panther Mountains beyond. Westward the Big Horn Mountain range continues its cragged front, past Piney summit and Rocky Face Ridge, until lost to view. Eastward, the Black Hills, beyond Reno, and Pumpkin Buttes, loom up at a distance of a hundred miles, and Rock Creek and Clear Fork are traced until they disappear in the buttes of the north. Southward, Cloud Peak rises sublimely, with its hoary head piercing the clouds and furnishing an exhaustless reservoir for the hungry streams below.

The ascent is slow and requires frequent rests. Animals as well as men pant under the strain; the breath becomes short and labored, giving no little pain with a sense of suffocation, and the perspiration drops from mules and horses as if they had just been lifted bodily from a complete emersion. But, when the topmost summit is attained, after threading the intricacies of a pine orchard half checked by young balsam and hemlock, the cup of coffee, with a sirloin of mountain sheep, cooked upon heated stones or spitted before the coals, acquire peculiar virtue and relish; and the mind never tires in study of the magnificent panorama disclosed.

The Big Piney itself is possessed of a variety of natural charms. The gorge through which the water rushes is nearly four hundred and fifty feet in height, and while the river soon buries itself in the pines below, so that the sighs of the winds through their branches are blended in solemn murmurs with the mad dash of cascades and the swift rush of the rapids, it often breaks out to the sunlight, and retains all its wildness and tumult of sounds, until it passes the fort, and, joined by its lesser sister, bears off for the Missouri through the intervening channels.

These are all rides for the saddle, although the ambulance can reach all but the mountain summit; and, until two narrow escapes, one on Big Piney and another beyond Pilot Hill, had taught the ladies the risk of exposure, it was no rare thing to see Mrs. Wands and others on a gallop for recreation and change.

The road from the fort to the Pinery is itself over the gentle southern slope of Sullivant Hills, and at the highest point before entering the woods, there is a fine view of Tongue River, the red buttes, and the lake, only surpassed by that of Fort Ridge itself.

Pilot Hill, only a few hundred yards from the fort, has its own fine views, and the traveler from Powder River can see, at the distance of eleven miles, its picket on the summit, watching for his arrival or keeping close scrutiny of the enemies of his peace.

The old road was abandoned the same week the site of the fort was selected; and though Colonel Sawyer soon after came over the old road as in 1865, all trains subsequently took the short cut-off from the lake to the fort.

Opposite the fort, a gradual slope, slashed by

occasional ravines, ends in a narrow table-land with another fine view of the fort, Peno valley, the mountains and the lake. In every direction are natural beauties which minister to the refined taste, and furnish, even at that distance from civilized life, such choice intercourse with nature, that separation from friends is softened and the hours of peace are like the moments of a pleasant dream.

The fort proper is six hundred feet by eight hundred, situated upon a natural plateau, so that there is a gradual slope from the front and rear, falling off nearly sixty feet in a few rods, thus affording a natural glacis, and giving to the position a positive strength, independent of other defenses A rectangle, two hundred by six hundred feet, is occupied by warehouses, cavalry stables, laundress quarters, and the non-commissioned staff.

About the parade-ground, already referred to, are officers' and men's quarters, offices, guard-house, sutler's and band building.

The stockade is made of heavy pine trunks eleven feet long, hewn to a touching surface of four inches so as to join closely, being pointed and loop-holed, and firmly imbedded in the ground for three feet. Block-houses are at two diagonal corners, and massive gates of plank with small wickets, all having substantial locks, are on three fronts, and on the fourth or southern

front, back of the officers' quarters, is a small gate for sallies, or for officers' use.

Three framed warehouses, the hospital and four company quarters, built in 1866, are eighty-four feet long and twenty-four feet wide, with ceilings of ten feet. The windows to soldiers' quarters, as well as those designed for officers, have three sashes each, giving ample light and cheerfulness to the whole garrison. Regulation bunks, with arm racks, shelves for knapsacks, boots, etc , are conveniently arranged, so that a company can form for roll-call between the two lines.

A flag-staff, surrounded by an octagonal band platform, stand, and seats, occupies, the center of the parade, and diverging walks, twelve feet wide, pass to each street, the magazine being in the center of one of the squares.

East of, and opening from the fort, extending with nearly an equal area, to the little Piney is the corral, or quartermaster's yard. This is surrounded by a rough cottonwood stockade, and contains stabling for mules, hay and wood yards, hay scales, quarters for teamsters and mechanics, the blacksmith, wagonmakers, carpenters, saddlers, and armorers' shops, and the general apparatus and conveniences of such a place.

From this corral, one gate opens toward the saw-mills, one toward the road from Powder River, and one to the clear waters of the Little

Piney, which here makes a convenient bend perfectly protected by the re-entering angle of the stockade just at that point.

Two steam saw-mills just above the mill gate, and but a few rods distant, furnish constant supplies of posts, plank, studding, rafters, lath and boards, and all lumber for every use.

The stockade of two thousand eight hundred feet circuit was completed in October, notwithstanding all other work and constant skirmishing went on, and, with the exception of most of the Sabbaths, there was no cessation of labor, whatever the weather, until the holidays of October 29th and 30th. On the first of November the same diligence was renewed, and each day's close was a new testimony to what a few men could accomplish under systematized labor and the will to work.

CHAPTER XVII.

TWO HOLIDAYS—OCTOBER INSPECTION AND REVIEW—FIRST GARRISON FLAG HOISTED IN ABSARAKA—INCIDENTS OF THE DAY—INDIAN RESPONSE TO A NATIONAL SALUTE—LOOKING-GLASSES IN ABUNDANCE—EVENING LEVEE.

THE last day of October being the stated day of Muster-for-pay, it was declared a holiday, as the previous day had been one of preparation. The completed flag staff was at last to receive its chief glory in flying the first garrison flag that ever rose over Absaraka.

The day was bright and lovely.

The whole command was in full dress, and after the inspection and review of the morning upon the plain before the fort, and the proper muster, the troops formed three sides of a square about the flag-staff, the fourth side having a platform for officers, ladies, and visitors, and the band taking station in the center.

Probably the programme would not conform closely to all conventionalisms of army usage, or find precise antecedents in army regulations, but it appeared to be designed more particularly to bring hard-working day-laborers back to something like military dress forms of parade, and supply a little recreation to those whose only in-

terval of rest was the occasional hours of sleep.
Shut out from civilized life, the only drawback
was the refusal of the colonel to let everybody
give some old-fashioned cheering when the work
was done. But all went off about as well as it
would elsewhere, and as it suited those whom it
was designed to gratify, it made no difference to
mankind at large.

Judge Kinney read an appropriate poem of
Miss Carmichael's chaste and spirited collection,
Chaplain White offered the prayer, and principal
musician Barnes, who, with William Daily, fashioned the flag-staff, presented to be read an original poem of his own, which at least did justice
to his patriotic spirit.

The following was the address, and is such a
brief resumé of the preceding work, and the results attained by the expedition of 1866 in a little more than three months of labor, that no
apology is made for its repetition, although already known to many:

"OFFICERS AND MEN,—Three and one-half
months ago stakes were driven to define the
now perfected outlines of Fort Philip Kearney.
Aggressive Indians threatened to exterminate
the command. Our advent cost us blood. Private Livensberger of Company F was the first
victim, July 17th, 1866; Lieutenant Daniels,
private Callery, of G Company; Gilchrist and

Johnson, of E Company; Fitzpatrick and Hacket, of D Company; Patrick Smith, of H Company; and Oberly and Wasser have also, in the order named, given their lives to vindicate our pledge to never yield one foot of advance, but to guarantee a safe passage for all who seek a home in the lands beyond.

"Fifteen weeks have passed, varied by many skirmishes and both night and day alarms, but that pledge holds good. In every work done your arms have been at hand. In the pine tracts or hay fields, on picket or general guard duty, no one has failed to find a constant exposure to some hostile shaft, and to feel that a cunning adversary was watching every chance to harass and kill.

"And yet that pledge holds good. Stockade and block-house, embrasure and loop-hole, shell and bullet, have warned off danger, so that women and children now notice the savage as he appears, only to look for fresh occasion for you to punish him, and with righteous anger to avenge the dead.

"The Indian dead outnumbers your own fourfold, while your acquired experience and better cause afford you constant success in every encounter. This is not all. Substantial warehouses, containing a year's supply, spacious and enduring quarters, and a well-adapted magazine are other proofs of your diligence and spirit.

"The steam whistle and the rattle of the mower have followed your steps in this westward march of empire. You have built a central post that will bear comparison with any for security, completeness, and adaptation to the ends in view, wherever the other may be located, or however long in erection.*

"Surrounded by temptations to hunt the choicest game, and allured by tales of golden treasure just beyond you, you have spared your powder for your foes, and have given the labor of your hands to your proper work. Passing from guard-watching to fatigue-work, and, after one night in bed, often disturbed, returning to your post as sentry; attempting with success all trades and callings, and handling the broad-axe and hammer, the saw and the chisel, with the same success as that with which you have sped the bullet, your work has proven how well deserved was the confidence I reposed in all of you; and that same old pledge still holds good.

"Coincident with your march to this point was the occupation of Fort Reno; first by Com-

---

* Brevet Brigadier General W. B. Hazen, upon his tour of inspection, pronounced this stockade to be the best he had ever seen, excepting only one in British America, built by the Hudson Bay Company, with great labor and expense. The previous description of Fort Philip Kearney is in substance derived from the *Army and Navy Journal* and *New York Times*.

pany B, afterward reinforced by Company F of this battalion, and the advance of Companies D and G to Fort C. F. Smith, nearly one hundred miles farther west. All these, like yourselves, having a share in the labor, the exposure, and the conflicts that throughout the whole length of the line attended its occupation, have sustained the past good record of the 18th Infantry, and thus also have vindicated your pledge.

"And now, this day, laying aside the worn and tattered garments, which have done their part during weeks of toil and struggle, the veteran battalion of the 18th Infantry, from which perhaps I shall soon be parted in the changes of army life and organization, puts on its fresh full-dress attire for muster and review.

"The crowning office, without which you would regard your work as scarcely begun, is now to be performed, and to its fulfillment I assign *soldiers;* neither discharging the duty myself, nor delegating it to some brother officer; but some veteran soldiers of good desert shall share with a sergeant from each of their companies, and the worthy man whose work rises high above us, the honor of raising our new and beautiful garrison flag to the top of the handsomest flag-staff in America.

"It is the first full garrison flag that has floated between the Platte and Montana; and this beautiful pole, perfect in detail, as if wrought and finished in the navy yards of New York, Philadelphia, or Boston, will be to Sergeant Barnes, whose appropriate and well-intended verses will be read to you, a long remembered trophy of his patriotism and skill; a new impulse to your own future exertions; a new cause for pride as its stripes and stars are daily unfolded; a new source of courage to each traveler westward advancing; and a new terror to foes who dare to assail you.

"With music and the roar of cannon we will greet its unfoldings.

"This day shall be a holiday, and a fresh starting-point for future endeavor.

"And yet, all is not said that I wish to say! While we exalt the national standard, and rejoice in its glory and its power, let us not forget the true source of that glory and power.

"For our unexampled health and continued success; for that land of the free and home of the brave; for our institutions and their fruits, we owe all to the Great Ruler who made and has preserved us.

"Let me, then, ask all, with uncovered heads and grateful hearts, to pause in our act of consecration while the chaplain shall invoke God's own blessing upon that act; so that while this banner rises heavenward, and so shall rise with each recurring sun, all hearts shall rise to the throne of the Infinite, and for this day, its duties and its pleasures, we shall become better men and better soldiers of the great Republic."

At the close of the prayer, the flag slowly rose to masthead, while national airs, the booming of cannon, and the sharp ring of *presented arms* paid it such tokens of respect as the occasion enjoined.

The afternoon was pleasant, and such recreation was indulged in as the men found agreeable. About three o'clock, Indians came out of the creek, and around the bend of Sullivant Hills, so quickly as to almost pass the west gate before they were discovered. They evidently hoped, by the suddenness of their movement, to cut off a few private horses that were grazing just south of the fort, but were disappointed. Others appeared upon the hills, and flashing mirrors were constantly passing signals for nearly an hour. It would seem as if the salute had attracted their attention, and they had supposed that other Indians were near the fort, or the white men had some other exhibition for their gratification and surprise. They had at least the pleasure of seeing the stars and stripes, and thus getting new hints as to the proposed length of our visit.

In the evening all the officers, in full dress, and the ladies of the garrison, attended the muster evening levee at the colonel's, where music, social dancing, and such an entertainment as was practicable, closed the day, and brought everybody up very closely to the grade of similar reunions in the States.

CHAPTER XVIII.

A DAY OF INCIDENTS—HOSTILE SIOUX AND FRIENDLY CHEYENNES—NARROW ESCAPE OF THE LATTER—OUR PICKET MIMICKED—MORE MASSACRES—CROQUET INTRODUCED INTO ABSARAKA.

ONE September morning was peculiarly bright and clear. A full moon had fairly invited the Indian deities to their best endeavor, but as a slight fall of snow half covered the earth all expectations of seeing red men gradually vanished from our minds. The timber train went as usual to the Pinery. A water party was at the larger creek before the fort. Details were at work on the ditch. Others were hewing, pointing, cutting loop-holes, or placing the completed trunks in the trenches. The saw-mills were busy, and men who had just come off guard cheerfully lent their energies to work upon their company barracks. The touch of snow seemed to hurry everybody. The band were just marching from the guard parade when an alarm was given.

We could all see, and, after the children were looked up or "accounted for," did our share of watching.

A party of seven Indians dashed out of the thick cottonwood at the confluence of the two Pineys and made boldly for the picket on Pilot Hill. It seemed that almost instantly the relief of the mounted picket, always saddled and ready, were out of the east gate upon a run, and yet it was plain that no riders or horses would be in time. The despised howitzers were brought into requisition, and a case shot was sent as a swifter messenger, with its relief of eighty bullets, and, as it hurtled through the air, the savages slackened speed a little to watch its advent. They found "the gun that shoots twice" too much for their dodging, and as its shell exploded over their heads, scattering its compliments and the earth in all directions, they turned their course and made for the brush as quickly as they had appeared. A second similar messenger dropped one Indian from the saddle, and all took to cover.

Directly opposite the fort, and only about seven hundred yards from the front gate, across the Piney, where Captain Bailey had encamped his party of miners, nearly fifty Indians made a dash for his horses; but the miners were quick as their foe, and were after them with revolvers and rifles; while again, "the gun that shoots twice" achieved a success. One Indian pony was shot by a miner, but, to our great disgust, his rider coolly leaped up behind another Indian and galloped off beyond the reach of harm.

A case shot and shell turned aside another party demonstrating from the west; but, simultaneously with the operations of these parties, a still larger force was spread out on the summit and slopes of Lodge Trail Ridge, just as if they had in view an attack upon the timber train while the other parties should skirmish and draw the attention of the garrison. A detachment was at once sent toward the woods, but the flashing looking-glasses all along the hills passed the quick signal that their plans had been foiled, and very soon all Indians had disappeared.

A messenger brought in word that Patrick Smith, belonging to the permanent block-house party in the woods, had dragged himself nearly a half mile to his camp, badly wounded with arrows, and scalped. He had managed to break off the shafts, so as not to be impeded in crawling through the thickets. Dr. Reid, Acting Assistant Surgeon, at once went to his relief; but he died within twenty-four hours.

While the working party were felling trees, a party of Indians broke through the woods and killed two of the detail who were a little separated from their comrades.

About two o'clock in the afternoon the sudden, repeated shriek of the steam-whistle at the farther mill, and the equally hasty signal of the pickets, gave the alarm that Indians were again close by. We could all see fifteen Indians between the fort and the mountain, galloping from the west directly for Pilot Hill, with the plain purpose of capturing and scalping the picket under the very eyes of the garrison. Before they had half ascended the hill, Captain Brown and Lieutenant Adair, with a party, were in hot pursuit. Private Rover (who is of good Chicago family, and enlisted under the false name of Rover) was in charge of the picket. He had been signally brave in several tight places before. On this occasion he dismounted his three men, turned the horses loose toward the fort with a good urging, and slowly fell off the northern slope, with arms at a "ready," to join the supporting party. The horses came down the steep grade toward the fort on a run, passing through the Indians, who dare not stop them and could only give them a few arrows as they passed. The chief warrior reached the summit, and for an instant turned his pony, to imitate the usual signal of riding in a circle until flags were used; but the pressure of Captain Brown's party soon put the Indians and their ponies to their mettle.

It was nearly night when the party returned, with wearied horses, to tell the tale of their adventures.

They brought with them a band of eight Cheyenne Indians and one squaw, whose broken-down ponies and miserable outfit showed that they were neither on the war-path nor very prosperous. It seems that Captain Brown, while pursuing the Sioux, saw them suddenly stop and have a short parley with a party coming from the east.

As the two separated, the latter came forward holding up a paper and showing themselves to be "Little Moon," "The Rabbit that Jumps," and "The Wolf that Lies Down," with a few others, on their way to the fort for provisions, and permission to go to Tongue River valley to hunt.

These chiefs were at the council in July, and said that Black Horse (who then was ill) was sick and in their camp at Rock Creek, and that old "White Head," the oldest living Cheyenne chief, was with them also: that they had been in the mountains as directed, and had crossed as far as Fort Caspar, where Brevet Major Morris had treated them well, and given them a letter to the colonel.

These Indians were permitted to camp on an island in Little Piney, under the notice of the saw-mill guard, and by dusk were cooking their bacon and coffee, which had been presented by Colonel Carrington.

Men of the timber train came in, and told the soldiers that some of this very party were with those who had killed Oberly and Wasser. This rumor spread through the garrison. Added to the fact that many officers and citizens had doubts whether some of the band of "Black Horse" were not among our active enemies, this developed a spirit of vengeance that soon made itself demonstrative.

It seemed too bad, when no man could go out of the stockade unarmed, and any negligence insured the most horrible death and torture, that any red man should be sheltered and fed by the garrison, its commander, or Colonel Carrington, the district commander.

About 9 o'clock Chaplain White called and said that the men talked about killing the Cheyennes; and soon after a soldier opened the door and said that "the men were killing the Indians." The colonel started at once, with revolver in hand, and three reports, soon after heard, showed that some issue had been made. As a matter of fact, nearly ninety men had quietly armed, and in the darkness of the night formed themselves opposite the Indians, cocked their pieces, all ready to fire, when a guard arrived and they were ordered back to post. Anxious not to be recognized when the guard arrived and they were ordered back, they disobeyed Captain Ten Eyck and rushed for the east gate; but the colonel's shots, after hesitation to obey his order to halt, stopped the party.

So far as the light could determine, they were found to be some of the best men of the garrison. They quickly realized the disgrace that would have fallen upon the post and regiment had they perpetrated the massacre, and for many reasons were restored to their barracks with only admonition and caution as to future conduct.

In fact, the next day these same Indians had a conference, and in the judgment of everybody vindicated their good faith by such information of their own movements and those of the Sioux, as fully comported with advices from other sources.

Old "White Head" also came, with a few braves, and had a talk with some of the officers; but the band, after the risk of the night before, and having been instructed to keep off the road (as soldiers could no longer discriminate when they met Indians on the road, or about the working parties), left us and returned no more.

Other days were as full of changing adventures as this. Few were without their share of less painful incidents. A game of croquet was planned, and while the ladies could neither ride nor walk beyond the gates, some amusement was attempted between Indian alarms; the evening found its recreation in the authors' game, a quiet quadrille, good music, conversation, and other varieties, besides the needle and cook-book.

It may be added, before this last reference to the Cheyennes, that when they were passed by the Sioux whom Captain Brown chased from Pilot Hill, the Sioux contemptuously struck them and cried "Coo!" as they did in July, when unable to induce the same party to engage in war against the whites and the occupation of the road.

CHAPTER XIX.

NIGHT SCENES—CELESTIAL AND TERRESTRIAL VISITORS—AURORA—LUNAR RAINBOW—METEORITES—INDIANS ALL IN THEIR WAR-PAINT.

The nights in Absaraka were peculiarly beautiful when cloudless. The rarity of the atmosphere gave full play to the star-beams, and it seemed as if there were twice as many as in any firmament elsewhere.

Their first appearance was often mistaken for Indian signal fires, as they rose above the horizon, like the sun or moon, having orbs as marked and light as brilliant as when they attained the zenith. In the glory of the full moon the snow-clad mountains shone as silver; while the deep roar of the cascades of Big Piney Fork was hardly less grateful to the wakeful soul than its lullaby was soothing to the weary.

From sunset until morning, this melody increased in power, as if making most of its time when man was not too busy to notice or enjoy, or as if seeking to comfort and quiet him after his day of toil. Each mid-day's thaw upon the mountains in summer would reach the great gates of exit just at that grateful hour when the undisturbed slumber is sweetest and soundest, and all natural harmonies intensify the blessing of morning sleep.

Now and then the aurora borealis put forth its pyrotechnic energies in a profuse variety of merry dances, vaulting streamers, and gorgeous coronas; and then, again, the lunar rainbow, with its strangely unreal tints and novelties, would banish sleep and bring us all to a patient attention to its claims, and thorough admiration of its wonderful characteristics.

August and November contributed their aerolites and proper share of meteors, and the blazing sky-path of these eccentric visitors shone fresh and clear after the celestial traveler had exploded itself, or had been otherwise disposed of under the laws of its being or the programme of the meteorologist and astronomer. Other nights were such as Æneas knew when the gods were angry, or Odin permitted when the storm-king was riding in state or in vengeance. *Then*, every mountain gorge had its own blast, and every gulch, ravine, and valley had its fitful and unruly current. Tent-flies took the proportions and direction of inflated balloons, and the snapping and flapping was suggestive of sky for the roofing and all out-doors for the inclosure of the habitation we dwelt in.

Such winds do justice to the theory and mission of winds. They blow as winds can only blow when in real earnest: and it is inflexibly certain that the classical Æolus of early times who used to cave and lock up the winds he was familiar with, never gained jurisdiction over the winds of Absaraka; or the whole history of his career and successes is simply a myth, or poetic fiction of by-gone days. In early school hours, when Madame M———s thought Latin was a special accomplishment as a basis of good English, we received the history and adventures of Æolus with as much faith as anybody did, and if compelled, at last, to question any alleged circumstances connected with his career, it is a matter of reluctant conviction, and not of captious skepticism as to the history of the past.

Other night scenes than those portrayed by Nature were frequently contributed by the native inhabitants of the land.

While the garrison were in tents few ladies slept soundly; and officers and men alike threw themselves down for repose as if expecting each moment a summons to duty. Beyond the general guard lines, the pickets were thrown out in several directions to watch for the approach of Indians; and as each relief went out it changed its station, so that enemies who knew the former position of the detail could not know its place two hours afterward. Scarcely had the post been located, when these night visitations became frequent.

On one occasion brisk firing was heard on all sides, and the entire garrison was under arms, while Lieutenant Adair's whole company was sent out to support the pickets and ward off attack. Numerous fancies often blended with the real facts, and false alarms alternated with the genuine. Thus, wonderful reports would come in of the flight of arrows that innocently whizzed past the men on duty; and yet the closest scrutiny by lantern or morning light would fail to discover the projectiles themselves. Sometimes a mule, straying from corral or parting his halter, became the victim of that constant vigilance which was the price of our lives and liberty; or sneaking wolves would be mistaken for sneaking Indians, whose habit of borrowing wolf-skins and wolf-cries to deceive us compelled instant attention to whatever had show of life. At other times crawling Indians would actually draw near enough to attempt a shot at the tents or sentries;

and at all times, dawn of day was the only sure indication that an enemy was not close at hand. One sign, however, became a fair one. When wolves were loudest and nearest, the Indians seldom were near; and the old trappers claimed to distinguish between the genuine wolf-howl and the Indian imitation by the fact that the former produced no echo. Either the natural or the imitated was ugly enough, and sufficiently abundant for that style of music.

With completion of the stockade the guard was reduced, and some sense of security prevailed. Until then, it is certain that any considerable body of Indians, with a proper leader, could have dashed through the camp and performed substantial mischief. But while the stockade kept Indians out, it did not keep them away. Still they ventured their shots at the sentries, fired arrows into the beef cattle close outside, and tried all possible measures to decoy and capture any who were imprudent and careless.

About nine o'clock one evening, a volley near the front gate aroused the garrison. Close to the stockade, and just at the foot of the natural slope which surrounds it, a small corral of wagons belonging to the sutler inclosed a group of teamsters engaged at cards. The first indication of the presence of Indians was a volley fired under the wagon beds, which wounded three, and one of them fatally. A detail from the guard was soon on the spot, and the low ground was scouted as far as the creek; but the night being dark, no Indians were found.

Another evening, just after taps, an alarm was given by the sutler that his stock, which had been left on herd half a mile south of the fort, on the Little Piney, was attacked; and besides his own men, Captain Brown, with forty infantry, moved out as skirmishers from that face of the fort toward the creek. Almost immediately a bright fire sprang up on the spur of Sullivant Hills, nearest the post on the west, around which the figures of Indians could be distinctly seen moving. The picket at the hay-ricks east of the fort, on Little Piney, fired two shots at horsemen on the creek, and there were other indications that several hostile parties were preying about us. The night was very dark, and objects could be seen but a short distance.

The bright fire, made up of pine flambeaus or torches, alone furnished any show of a fair target, and received complimentary attention.

A careful range was given to the field howitzer, loaded with a twelve-pound spherical case shot, and three twelve-pound mountain howitzers were also loaded and trained in three other directions, where there was any probability of stirring up the skulkers. All were discharged at one word, and the first shell exploded directly over the fire, scattering its bullets and the Indians as well, while the fire was instantly extinguished and the night passed without further interruption. The stock were brought in safely, with the report that the Indians abandoned their game as soon as the party on the hills was scattered. It evidently was a novel surprise, that at night, and at the distance of several hundred yards, the white soldiers could reach them with such plentiful volleys as a case shot distributes.

The duties of the officer of the day at night were always exacting and full of incident; and indeed, while every day brought its probabilities of some Indian adventures near the fort or at the Pinery, every night had its special dangers, which unanticipated might involve great loss, if not the sacrifice of the post, its garrison, and stores.

Repeated attempts were made to approach the large hay-ricks for the purpose of setting them on fire; and while as a general rule large parties only appeared at the full of the moon, the forays of stealing and scalping bands were constantly harassing and probable.

Such demonstrations were seldom early in the evening. Just at daybreak, when sleep is soundest, and the faintest glimmer of light discloses unprotected stock or exposed positions, was the favorite hour with the sharp red man.

Two days after Captain Fetterman arrived,

impressed with the opinion, to which he had often given language, that "a company of regulars could whip a thousand, and a regiment could whip the whole array of hostile tribes," he was permitted to make the experiment of lying in the cottonwood thickets of Big Piney from two o'clock until ten o'clock in the morning, using hobbled mules for live bait to decoy the aborigines.

A beautiful Sunday morning dawned, and no Indians were seen; and so close was the covert that the glass did not reveal the secreted party. About nine o'clock Mrs. Wheatley rode in front of the fort with Mr. Reid, passing it nearly a half mile, where her husband's cattle were feeding, and at least a mile from the expected skirmish. The team soon came back upon the run, some Indians having dashed forth, driven off the cattle, and not capturing the wagon and passengers because of a presented rifle, or the assurance that the stock was theirs at all events, while a moment's delay would expose them to quick pursuit from the fort. The Indians may or may not have known the plan for their surprise; but their sagacity and suspicion, their keen sight, and knowledge of woodcraft are seldom at loss; and while they were often foiled and disappointed, or repulsed with loss, they were always innocent of being surprised, and shrewdly made their own advances so covered that they were near the desired object before their presence was known.

So it was that nights in Absaraka, so cool and suggestive of sweetest sleep, were associated with wakefulness and danger; and at least one officer, whose responsibilities were as large as any, slept for weeks in succession without removal of garments, and nightly made his rounds to secure personal knowledge of the deportment of the guard and the condition of the post.

Habit, however, soon accustomed those who were not immediately on duty to trust the vigilance of the guard, and to sleep by snatches that grateful sleep which elsewhere never could be beat.

was above everything reasonable in a household, and that a fortune was soon to be realized by selling villainous pies to soldiers at half a dollar or more for a pie.

Ladies found themselves obliged to turn milliners and dressmakers; and we know experimentally that our experience in fabricating boys' clothes alone was worth a good apprenticeship, if it should ever become necessary to rush to a trade for support.

Frank Leslie's and Madame Demerest's magazine became each a desideratum, and linsey-woolsey, delaines, and calico nowhere else underwent such endowment with fashionable shapes as in Absaraka. Darning and stitching, hemming and hemstitching, cutting and basting were as inevitable as the need of clothes to wear. The triplet of "I never could, I never would, and I never will," became almost obsolete; and in their place was these other impulses, "I wouldn't, but I must and I will," or "I could, I can, and I *do!*" Unhappy were any who despised to begin, and, in the penalty of charcoal beefsteak, hot water soups, and dyspeptic biscuit, were driven to despair or disgust.

But any life on the plains is a good school, and its practical suggestions take all the starch and false pride as to work completely out of the unfortunate human creature who expects the spoon to be carried to the mouth by attendants,

CHAPTER XX.

DOMESTIC, SOCIAL, AND RELIGIOUS LIFE, WITH THE EPISO\
THEREIN OCCURRING.

WOMAN had a choice field in Absaraka for the exercise of many industrial pursuits, and fortunate were those who in earlier days had been advised that other rooms than the parlor have their uses, and other fingering than that of the piano must be employed in roasting and boiling, in frying and broiling, in baking and stewing. It was found that yeast was to be made before the bread could be extra, that the hands were to be servants when no other servants could be had; and it was discovered by some that the dish-cloth and wash-cloth, the broom and the duster were susceptible of as graceful manipulation as prinking irons, or the strings of lute and guitar. In fact, every morning brought its round of ante-breakfast labor, with that restoring process by which dishes once used are brought back to proper condition for future uses. Female servants were scarce, independent, and disputant. The few taken with families had learned that their market value for washing and a metropolitan table to be spread by the hands of a striker.

Primitive ways are to be learned; but the tent becomes neat and genteel, and the taste of its arrangement and adornment gives capital hints to the mind of the beauty of patience, and especially confirms the sacred maxim, that content with godliness is great gain.

The snapping of a tent-pole at midnight under three feet of snow; the blaze of the canvas, as the ambitious fire commissions the red-hot pipe to unroof your earthly tabernacle, at no small risk to bedding and trunks; the pretty little drifts that gracefully slip through the closely drawn entrance and sprinkle your bed, your furniture, and your wardrobe, all afford change and excitement, and not unseldom bring occasion to begin housekeeping anew. The frozen-up kettles, pots, and buckets demand recognition; while the milk, the cream, and the butter are incentives to new branches of industry and skill.

So when houses are used, one house will differ from another house in glory. The adobe, with its unplastered surface, and the dropping of dirt from the earth-covered roof, is one variety; and the log-cabin is another variety; either of which involves much ingenuity, not to say genius, as the mind struggles to give them neatness and comfort. Yet either of these soon becomes home; and its protection from summer's heat and winter's cold is often more grateful and complete than more pretending edifices of wood or brick. It is indeed not always easy to adapt a carpet to dirt floors, or the changing sizes of army habitations; nor is it pleasant to break up and begin housekeeping several times a year. Always there is something you cannot carry with you, something which must be sold or given away. *Always* some favorite chair is broken and crockery mysteriously disappears, requiring new outlay at prices beyond reason, and trying the patience and temper by sound and certain tests. Custom familiarizes the different styles, shapes, and colors of plates and dishes, as they are replenished at different times and places; but while the tin-cup and plate are *splendid* on the march, they do not come up to the ideal of comeliness and elegance in preparation for a reception or dinner-party given to strangers.

When, after a successful trip of six hundred miles, our two cows were driven away one Sunday afternoon by some very mean Indians, there ensued another of those episodes which distract the mind and mar all plans as to butter and cream for cake and for coffee. The wolves took our nice turkey hen just as she was ready to give us a brood of little turkeys; while half of our young chickens in that bracing climate gaped themselves to death. Yet, with all these sacrifices and losses from repeated change, there were real cosey times in tents, houses, or in cabins. The good nature and good sense of Uncle Samuel had furnished canned provisions, greatly to our personal comfort and pecuniary convenience; but fresh vegetables were most precious and rare. A few potatoes from Bozeman City, sent with the regards of Brevet Lieutenant-Colonel Kinney, were a great treat; and Major Almstedt, paymaster, was good enough to spare a half cabbage and eleven onions, through one of his trips, to astonish the palate, and minister to a craving for something novel from the United States. Ingenuity was tasked to invent new cookery for cove oysters and other savory preserved edibles; and wild plums, gooseberries, currants, grapes, and cherries furnished a preserve *basis* quite palatable and natural.

Wild meats would have been abundant; but the stringent Indian game laws of that country treated all hunting by the white man as poaching, and the preserves were skillfully guarded, to cut off so far as possible every impulse to trespass.

Evenings had their readings, their games, and quiet quadrilles. Music was a never-failing relief for body and mind; and the interchange of patterns, books, and receipts kept up material for new industry and new themes for deliberation or chit-chat. Sickness, though rare, brought its sympathies, and its little interchange of good things and delicacies; and with the occasional pressure of unsatisfied longings there was developed a peculiarly apt illustration of the idea that people really don't want much of anything, and the Scripture was confirmed that "a man's life consisteth not in the abundance of what a man possesseth."

Change and frequent parting brought those peculiar separations that nowhere else are so tender as in army life on the frontier. Captain Haymond, Lieutenants Phisterer and D'Isay left us for recruiting service only two weeks after we reached our destination; and subsequently, Lieutenant Adair and Lieutenant Bisbee, wife and child. Others came, and quite a coterie shared in the round of evening sociables, which relieved the tension of continual excitement, and brought into being some features similar in kind to those of by-gone times at home.

Nor was the Sabbath neglected. Each new building, that was available in turn, became our sanctuary, as there was not time to build exclusively for chapel purposes. The sutler's store, the commissary building, company headquarters, and the band pavilion of evergreens successively shared the honor. The string band accompanied the voices, and, far away from the church-going bell and the heaven-directing spires, the praise of God was sung and Divine help implored. Few are the sanctuaries in civilized states where the *"Magnificat," "Gloria in Excelsis," "There is a light in the window," "Old Hundred,"* and *"Coronation"* were supported by a better orchestra or sung with more spirit.

The garrison itself had its own occasional social gatherings; and such was the general sobriety, the patient obedience and thorough absorption of the men in the plans of their commander, that drunkenness was rare and profanity less than usual. The stringent orders against verbal or personal abuse, the public reprimand administered on one occasion, and the governing principle that while obedience must be cheerful and immediate, the rights of the soldier as a man must be regarded, inspired the men with confidence and new ambition to fulfill their full measure of duty.

CHAPTER XXI.

INDIAN WARFARE—THINGS A WOMAN CAN LEARN WHEN SHE HAS SEEN THEM TRIED.

When even a woman shares the contingencies of entering a new country with troops, she must learn something besides the lessons of housewifery, endurance, and patience.

When days, weeks, and months pass with constantly recurring opportunities of seeing Indians in small and in large parties dashing at pickets, driving in wood parties, harassing water details, and, with dancing and yelling, challenging the garrison to pursuit; when, now and then, one, two, or more casualties mark the issues of a day, and these culminate, until at last five wagon-loads of bodies give evidence of the cunning barbarity and numbers of the foe; when night alarms are common, and three men are shot within thirty yards of the gates; when the stockade becomes a prison-wall, and over its trunks are seen only the signs of precaution or active warfare; when the men are never idle, but all are daily engrossed in essential labor, with no signs of reinforcement or aid; when the usual thankless task of opening a new country with its uncertainties and enmities, with resources absurdly deficient, meets only obloquy and abuse for the principal actors, she acquires *somehow*, whether by instinct or observation, it matters not which, an idea that Indians *will fight*, and sometimes do become quite wicked and dangerous. Surely, their ways are not as our ways, and their ponies are not like our horses. Their commissariat and their forage are not in trains or on pack mules; their campaigns are not extensively advertised in advance, nor do they move by regular stages or established routes.

Yes, even a woman, after several hundred miles of journey alternately in the ambulance or side saddle, sometimes in corral expecting its aid for safety, and again in the winding defile, where the very place excites the keenest scrutiny and is suggestive of noble red men with the nobility ignored, will see some peculiarities of Indian warfare when Indians are really venomous, and will draw conclusions for friends to consider, even if they only elicit a smile at her timidity, simplicity, or weakness.

James, the novelist, never compelled his solitary horseman to fight a Sioux, and, had the Knight of the Leopard, at the Diamond of the Desert, met more than one quiver of the darts of the Saracen, his adventures might have ended while his career was scarcely begun. Not unlike the Arab is the Indian of the Northwest. Isolated, yet in communication through the little mirrors which flash the sunlight and pass his signals for miles; separated, yet by the lance, pennon, and flags combined, when opportunity is inviting; dashing directly forward at a run, with the person crouched on the pony's neck, and wheeling only to throw himself out of sight and pass his arrows and bullets under the animal's neck before he returns for a fresh venture; fleeing everywhere, apparently at random, so that his pursuer must take choice of object of quest only to find his hot pursuit fruitless, with gathered numbers in his line of retreat; shooting up and down red buttes, where the horse of the white man breaks down at once; running on foot, with the trotting pony just behind him seeking a rest from the burden of his master; imitating the cry of the wolf and the hoot of the owl, when it will hide his night visit,—these Indians are everywhere, where you suppose they are not; and are certain to be nowhere, where you suppose them to be, sure.

In ambush and decoy, *splendid;* in horsemanship, *perfect;* in strategy, *cunning;* in battle, *wary* and careful of life; in victory, jubilant; and in vengeance, fiendish and terrible.

Too few to waste life fruitlessly; too superstitious to leave their dead to the enemy; too cunning or niggardly of resources to offer fair fight; too fond of their choice hunting-grounds to yield willing possession to the stranger,—they wait and watch, and watch and wait, to gather the scalps of the unwary and ignorant, and bear off their trophies to new feasts, new orgies, and new endeavor.

So reluctant are they to attack a foe under cover, that during the year 1866—once before stated—not a train was lost or seriously embarrassed when in corral; nor was any considerable party assailed when it sought judicious and substantial defense. Yet, daring and watchful, none better estimate the foe they contend with. When white men have delivered their fire, and the gleam of the ramrod has shown that the single-shooting arm was in use, then follows the wild dash, with revolvers and arrows, so quick and so spirited that their loss is as nothing, and swift ponies take them safely away for renewal of attack. Circling and intermingling to confuse all aim, affecting retreat seemingly to break up their array, and by some ravine, gulch, cañon, or thicket to appear on fresh and better vantage-ground, they approximate ubiquity, and fill the terse discription of the veteran Bridger, "Where there ain't no Injuns, you'll find 'em thickest."

Good judges of numbers, and quick to estimate the strength and designs of an enemy; keen to maintain their scouts and secure due notice of reinforcements; rarely, though sometimes, fighting in masses, but then with such involved and concerted disorder as to insure their purpose, when the plan is to overwhelm alive and capture for the torture,—this same Indian must find in his final master a better-armed and well-disciplined foe, who has studied his country and his nature, and this before his peace-offerings will be abiding and honest, or his hunting-grounds shall become the peaceful path of the traveler.

With all this, these same Indians have read the book of fate, and in the establishment of mutually supporting and well-garrisoned strongholds they will be foiled as to protracted interruption of emigration and travel. When this end is reached, and the great route through Absaraka is occupied and guarded, the game will flee the range of the white man's rifle, and the desperate Indian must abandon his home, fight himself to death, or yield to the white man's mercy.

Fired by the progress of the settler and the soldier; seeing as never before the last retreat of the buffalo, the elk, and the deer invaded by a permanent intruder; looking at his rights as violated, and the promises of many agents as unfulfilled; taught by nature, if not by the white man, that he is the lawful tenant of the waste he roams over until he has bartered his right away,—he has some reason to exclaim, as Red Cloud assured Black Horse, when the latter, in July, 1866, said, " Let us take the white man's hand and what he gives us, rather than fight him longer and lose all,"— the answer was: "White man lies and steals. My lodges were many, but now they are few. The white man wants *all*. The white man must fight, and the Indian will die where his fathers died."

Growing conscious of the white man's power, knowing how vain is an open field struggle, they avoid such determining issues, and waylay in detail, gradually enlarging their sphere of action, and thereby gathering in the young men and disaffected of other bands, until common cause may be had of all whose wrongs or temper inspire them to keep the war-path longer.

The frequent change of dwelling-place in a great area of hunting-ground gives them peculiar aptitude for this warfare and peculiar immunity from punishment. A single pony will bear and drag the lodge poles of a tepah, and the squaws will not only relieve the warriors of all menial details, but with the old men and boys are no despicable protectors of a village when the fighting men are in pursuit of game or scalps.

Thus Indian fighting is no parade of ceremony specifically described in regulations, nor an issue between fair and generous opponents. It is at all times destruction for the white man to fail, and his exposures, his perils, and even his successes, so much less heralded and estimated than in more artificial war with those of his own race, only bring him the personal consciousness of duty done to balance wasting years, loss of social life, and a bare support. With all this, and the sometimes recurring feeling of bitterness prompting the desire to exterminate his foe and thereby visit upon him some of the horrid scenes he has passed through, there comes the inevitable sentiment of pity, and even of sympathy with the bold warrior in his great struggle; and in a dash over the plains, or breathing the pure air of the mountains, the sense of freedom and independence brings such contrast with the machinery and formalities of much that is called civilized life, that it seems but natural that the red man in his pride and strength should bear aloft the spear-point, and with new resolve fight the way through to his final home in the Spirit land.

CHAPTER XXII.

INDIAN ARMS, HABITS, AND CUSTOMS—THE ARROW BEATS THE REVOLVER.

POPULAR opinion has regarded the Indian bow and arrow as something primitive and well enough for the pursuit of game, but quite useless in a contest with the white man. This idea would be excellent if the Indian warriors would calmly march up in line of battle and risk their masses so armed against others armed with the rifle. But the Indian comes as the hornet comes, in clouds or singly, yet never trying to sting until his ascendency is assured and his own exposure is slight.

At fifty yards a well-shapen, iron-pointed arrow is dangerous and very sure. A handful drawn from the quiver and discharged successively will make a more rapid fire than that of the revolver, and at very short range will farther penetrate a piece of plank or timber than the ball of an ordinary Colt's navy pistol.

The arrow-head varies in length and shape, and the shaft itself slightly changes, according to the tastes of different bands or tribes; and yet so constantly are arrows exchanged in gambling or barter that the character of the arrow used does not invariably determine the tribe engaged. Such were many of the arrows taken from the bodies of Captains Fetterman, Brown, Lieutenant Grummond, and others, after the massacre of December, 1866. All the peculiarities there found have been seen in the quivers of the Kittekehas, Chowees, Petropowetaws, and other Pawnees, all of whom are friendly, and some of whom are now, as in the winter of 1865–6, in the employ of the United States. The head is often barbed, but not generally, and is from two to three and a half inches in length, made of iron, and ground to a double edge. The shaft, which is about twenty-five inches in length, is winged by three feathers of the eagle, sage-hen, or wild-goose, and from the sinew wrapping of the head to that which binds the feathers is deeply marked by three grooves or blood-seams, so that when the flesh of man or beast closes about the shaft, these seams act as conduits and gradually bleed the victim to death. These grooves are with some Indians straight, and with others are zigzag or winding from midway down to the feathers.

The bows of Ogillalla and Brulè Sioux, Arrapahoes, Cheyennes, and most of the Indians east of the Rocky Mountains, are from thirty-two to forty inches long, of great elasticity and tension, so that they easily drive an arrow through a two-inch plank, and even through a man or buffalo.

The hatchet is generally that which is furnished by Indian agents or traders, often having the head and handle hollow and connected for use as a pipe; and, when possible, the handle itself is profusely studded with brass nails such as once distinguished parlor sofas and chairs.

Rifles, both English and American, abound. The "Hawkins" is a favorite, carrying what is called the "trade ball," and requiring a patch; but many of the old guides, trappers, and half-breeds still cling to their use as in the days of Pathfinder and other heroes of Cooper.

The quiver and bow-case are made of deerskin, bearskin, otter and other hides, or furs; and the armament of Hawkeye, which now hangs before the writer, is elaborate with tassels and pendants from well-dressed beaver.

The shield is worn by many of the leading braves, and is formed of several thicknesses of hide fastened through and through about the edge with sinew, and studded with brass nails, or ornamented with silver and other bright metal.

The spear varies from five and a half to seven feet in length, having a head nearly eighteen inches long, with a small pennon; and the heel of the shaft is balanced with eagle feathers, while others are caught along the shaft, giving steadiness to the flight, and suiting the diversified tastes of the owner.

The right and left hair of the warrior or brave is brought before the ear, braided or twisted, and wrapped with strings or ribbons, and falling upon the breast; while a third braid, falling behind and below the scalp-lock or tuft, often is covered with a succession of silver medallions hammered from coin, gradually diminishing in size from four inches to one inch as the series approaches the ground.

Earrings, necklaces, bracelets, and armlets are of brass, beads, bears' claws, or silver, but more generally of beautiful combinations of shells from the Pacific, seventy-five of which have been the price of a pony, and show the close relations of trade maintained between the tribes of the opposite slopes of the Rocky Mountains.

Moccasins, leggings, breech-cloth, and a buffalo robe belted about the waist, leaving the breast bare, is the sole dress of the majority. Others have jackets more or less fancifully decorated with small bullet buttons, and every article of dress that an American soldier uses is at once assumed when its possession is acquired. Trowsers are, however, cut off at the hip, as their own style of protection is habitually preferred. Gifts of clothing are quickly put on; and a present of gentlemen's underclothes once given to a Pawnee was so quickly substituted for his original garments as barely to allow escape from the room during the process.

The women vary little in costume except in a wrapping something like a petticoat or skirt, but wear less paint. The hair-parting is, however, invariably painted vermilion when visiting or in full dress, and cheeks, chin, and arms have their share of brilliant tints. Warriors, squaws, and children alike use the bow and arrow, but the women are peculiarly apt with knife and hatchet. The youngsters have a javelin exercise which is admirably fitted to prepare them for their future life. A small hoop is held by the thumb and forefinger of the right hand, while within the hand is the spear. The hoop is thrown forward on the ground, and the javelin is sent after and through the ring with great dexterity and success. This, with the cast of the hatchet and play of the knife, takes the place of the white boy's baseball or marbles; and the blunt-headed arrow brings down birds and small game that would be spoiled by the keener shaft.

The revolver is becoming quite common, and is used with more dexterity and skill than is the rifle. The following instance will illustrate a remarkable failure in rifle firing. Soon after Captain Fetterman arrived, he rode to the Pinery with Lieutenant Bisbee, Captain Ten Eyck, and one or two other officers who had just arrived, to see the locality. They descended to Pine Island just after the last timber-wagon had come out on the road, and in advance of their escort. They were received by a volley of from fifteen to twenty rifle shots, which were fired from a rest upon a fallen tree, at a distance of only fifty paces, as actually measured, without injury to anybody. A second volley equally failed to touch a man. A little bugle-boy brought word to the garrison that all were killed, for he saw the Indians as they fired and the officers as they disappeared. They were compelled to skirmish down the island before they could extricate themselves from the dilemma. A supporting party went out, but met them returning, and thus relieved the anxiety of the garrison.

The Indians not only use mirrors and flags for signal purposes, but many carry with them good field and spy-glasses, some of English styles, procured from Canada, and others are supplied by traders on the frontier.

The domestic life of the Indian, with the barbarity of the sun-dance and the filth of his home, have been often described; but the plenitude of furs in the land of Absaraka have furnished peculiar facilities for adornment and somewhat better wardrobes than are usual nearer the Lower Missouri and Mississippi waters. Their tepah (tepee, or lodge) is the model from which the Sibley tent was derived, and will accommodate several families; but nothing else on the face of the earth will furnish a more curious medley of contents than does a tepah where two or three families, of all ages and sizes, with all their worldly goods and hopes are huddled, piled, and crammed about its fire, and where the fitful wind and lazy squaws are combined in the effort to smoke buffalo tongues, strips of meat, and *Injun* all together. The picture is complete, by way of contrast, if a kettle of boiling water over the fire has received a fat dog just after his throat felt the knife, and a white officer, on a pile of furs, is doing his best to show how gracefully he can endure the honors and dinner specially designed for his presence. All this, too, while other officers and ladies are cheerfully waiting outside in the glad consciousness of escape from the hospitality of a chief.

Bells, triangles, and common horns have found their way among these Indians, and they eagerly adopt from the white man whatever makes noise or show.

CHAPTER XXIII.

MASSACRE OF LIEUTENANT BINGHAM—ACCOUNTS GIVEN BY OFFICERS—EXTRACTS FROM JOURNAL.

FORT PHILIP KEARNEY, December 6th, 1866. I hardly know how to take up my sadly interrupted journal. This day, with its bright morning, brought its sweet promise of rest from Indian alarms, and throughout the garrison all work was pushed with vigor; but the evening adds another sad chapter to the history of our frontier life.

The garrison waited anxiously until nearly nine o'clock before the distant bugle-note indicated the return of parties which, since nine in the morning, have been in pursuit of Indians. It seems hardly possible that poor Bingham, the gentle, manly, and soldierly young officer, who has already won the esteem of everybody, has already, so soon after his arrival, fallen a victim to his ardor and the craft of our foes. It seems that such a disaster has been necessary, to check the natural impulse of every one who comes here to chase Indians regardless of number or rules. Mr. Grummond and Mr. Wands have given me the whole history, and it is of God's mercy that any one escaped. Captain Fetterman has been in, and says "he has learned a lesson, and that this Indian war has become a hand-to-hand fight, requiring the utmost caution," and he wants no more such risks.

When the Indians attacked the wood train in the morning, Captain Fetterman was sent with mounted infantry and a part of Lieutenant Bingham's cavalry to drive the Indians over Lodge Trail Ridge, while the colonel, with Lieutenant Grummond and about twenty-five or thirty mounted men, crossed Big Piney to intercept the party chased by Captain Fetterman. Nearly two hundred Indians were in front of Captain Fetterman, hotly engaging his party, when fifteen of the cavalry, with Lieutenant Bingham, left him, for some reason unknown to everybody. The colonel's party pushed for the scene of action, and met the cavalry dismounted on one of the forks of Peno, but without Mr. Bingham. It seems that he had dashed westward after he saw the colonel's party galloping down the hills, and Mr. Grummond, by some sudden impulse, was led to leave his own party and join Mr. Bingham, both disappearing suddenly and nearly alone.

The colonel's party followed down the valley, according to original plan, until the opening below showed a large force of Indians beyond, and fast gathering on the flanks. Only seven men and a bugle-boy turned the point with him, and Indians were constantly circling around to draw their fire. Private McGuire's horse went down with him, as he gratefully tells his story, and an Indian was crawling along to scalp him, when the party stopped for him and he was lifted up. The recall was sounded, and Corporal Baker hearing it rode over a hill from the north, reporting that Lieutenant Bingham had certainly gone beyond the second hill, though just then there were at least eighty Indians in sight before that hill. Soon after Captain Fetterman came up, having crossed over to the other party after the defection of the cavalry, and a movement was made at once for the rescue of Lieutenant Bingham. Lieutenant Wands, who had superseded Captain Brown as regimental quartermaster, was to have started with the colonel, but being delayed to exchange his horse, by mistake joined the other party. He had been grazed by a ball, and probably his coolness and his Henry rifle saved that detachment after Lieutenant Bingham left it, as the others fired revolvers, even at several hundred yards, and Lieutenant Bingham threw his away.

The party rode but a few rods on the hill when suddenly a shout was heard: "For God's sake, come down quick," and through a gulch where the road was visible seven Indians were seen with their spear-heads close upon the backs of four of our men, one of whom was Lieutenant Grummond.

Mr. Wands thinks, from the formation of the ground, that had they passed that ravine a moment sooner or later, they would have seen nothing of Mr. Grummond's party until they should have found their bodies on return.

A few moments later the body of Lieutenant Bingham was found, and that of Sergeant Bowers, who was still living, though his skull was cleft through with a hatchet. He had killed three Indians with his revolver before he was overpowered. Private Donovan, always so brave, was with the party. They had been surrounded by thirty Indians while Lieutenants Grummond and Bingham were pursuing a dismounted Indian and cutting at him with sabers.

An ambulance was sent for, and Captain Arnold went out with forty men to reinforce the party. The remains of Lieutenant Bingham are in hospital, to be cared for and prepared for burial.

* * * * * *

December 9th, 1866. Lieutenant Bingham and Sergeant Bowers were buried to-day. Lieutenant Grummond conducted the masonic services, assisted by Mr. Weston, Mr. Saunders, Mr. Beckwith and others, while Chaplain White conducted the religious portion.

Thus our cemetery fills up with only the victims of violence! Everything in nature is so beautiful, and the climate is so restoring and healthful, that one could look upon such frontier life with something like complacency were it not for these savages, or even if the long and anxiously expected reinforcements could be seen or heard from. Sometimes it seems as if nobody cared if we had help or not.

Sergeant Bowers was such a favorite with Captain Brown that he placed his own corps-badge upon the breast of the remains; and the men feel especially vindictive and anxious for revenge, as Bowers had so often led the hay parties and successfully skirmished in defense of their work.

The officers feel more than ever the necessity of completing all necessary work and preparing for winter, and many believe that we may shortly expect, as the Crows indicated, the return of Indians in still larger force, to try and cut off work and supplies, if they do not dare to come near the fort and attempt its capture by surprise.

After the funeral, Lieutenant Grummond came in to speak of the services at the grave, which were very impressive, and again expressed his gratitude for his preservation. The lesson will not be lost, and shows what madness it is to follow these Indians very far with insufficient force, and what great peril may come to the post and whole line of road by rash impulses and disregard of the special work that presses so hard.

We think now that we shall not soon hear from Fort C. F. Smith, as Lieutenant Bingham had just returned from that post, having an escort of twenty-five men; and Brevet Lieutenant-Colonel Kinney, who has just made us a week's visit, thinks it unsafe to undertake the trip with less than an escort of fifty good men.

Our mail is overdue, and no doubt the courier and mail party are detained as guides to troops. The sentries understand they are not to fire at messengers coming from the east, and we shall soon have letters and papers after a long intermission. Perhaps the news of our difficulties has by this time been received, and nearly six months of trial may be succeeded by six months of triumph. We learn, as did Crusoe, how much can be done during comparative isolation from a civilized world.

CHAPTER XXIV.

FETTERMAN'S MASSACRE—ITS LESSONS.

December, 21st, 1866, was to us the saddest day of the year. Though snow covered the mountains, and there was every indication of the return of severe weather, the morning was quite pleasant. Men only wore blouses at their work, and the train, although much later than usual, went to the Pinery with a strong guard, so that the teamsters, choppers, and escort, all armed, numbered not far from ninety men.

The children ran in about 11 o'clock, shouting "Indians!" and the pickets on Pilot Hill could be distinctly seen giving the signal of "many Indians," on the line of the wood road; and news was also furnished that the train was in corral only a short distance from the garrison.

The officers and all the ladies were soon watching for other usual demonstrations, while a detail was being organized to relieve the train.

Brevet Lieutenant-Colonel Fetterman, then walking back and forth before his quarters, near where the colonel was giving his instructions, asked and obtained permission to go with the detachment.

Lieutenant Grummond, also at his own request, took a part of Company C, 2d United States Cavalry,—making the whole force just seventy-eight officers and men. Captain Brown, unknown to the officers of the garrison, as well as citizens Wheatley and Fisher, both experienced frontiersmen and good shots, also joined the party.

It was just at the time when a few more trains of saw-logs would furnish ample lumber material to complete the office building and a fifth company quarters, already well under progress.

The orders were given in front of Lieutenant Grummond's house, next the colonel's, and those who were present heard them repeated with distinctness and special urgency. Lieutenant Wands was also instructed to repeat them. As if peculiarly impressed with some anticipations of rashness in the movement, the colonel, just after the command left, went across the parade-ground to a sentry platform, halted the mounted party, and gave additional orders, understood in the garrison, and by those who heard them, to be the substantial repetition of the former.

The health of Mrs. Grummond was such that Lieutenant Wands and other friends urged him, for his family's sake, to be prudent, and avoid all rash movements and any pursuit that would draw them over Lodge Trail Ridge, and to report to Brevet Lieutenant-Colonel Fetterman the orders he had received. These orders were, in so many words, "to relieve the train, and under no circumstances to cross the ridge." Everybody knew why special emphasis was given to these orders.

Only two days before, Brevet Major Powell had been sent out to relieve a train, and obeyed his orders literally, although, as he afterward said, he was sorely tempted to pursue, but became afterward convinced that certain destruction would have been the result. Major Powell was in fact assigned to command the relieving party on the 21st; but when Brevet Lieutenant-Colonel Fetterman stepped forward and claimed it by seniority of rank, he was permitted to go and received his instructions.

The day before, and succeeding that on which Major Powell had reported several hundred Indians present, the colonel himself took charge of trains to the Pinery, spending the day in building a bridge over the creek and superintending the chopping parties and guard detail. All the indications were that the numerous Indian villages on Tongue River would lose no chance to do mischief, and the garrison was insufficiently supplied with arms, even of old styles, for the men actually at the post. Before Captain Fetterman left, a few Indian pickets were seen on Lodge Trail Ridge, and a few were below the fort at the road crossing. Two or three case shot, dropped near them, dismounted one and brought nearly thirty out of the brush. These at once disappeared. After the detachment had been gone a short time, finding that Captain Fetterman had left without a surgeon, the colonel sent Dr. Hines, with one of his own orderlies, to join the train and report to Captain Fetterman; Doctor Hines started, but soon returned with the news that the train had safely pursued its route to the woods; that Captain Fetterman was on the ridge to the north, out of view, and that there was so many Indians in sight that he could not join the party. It was about noon, and a man rushed in to say that firing was renewed. Every shot could be heard, and there was little doubt that a desperate fight was going on in the valley of Peno Creek beyond the ridge. The presence of Lieutenant Grummond with the party gave us new anxiety, and many heartfelt prayers were offered that he might return in safety. The colonel was on the "lookout," on headquarters building, and gave his orders before coming down.

It seemed long, but was hardly twelve minutes before Captain Ten Eyck, Lieutenant Matson, Dr. Hines, and Dr. Ould, with a relieving party, were moving, on the run, for the scene of action. We had all watched Captain Fetterman until the curve of Sullivant Hills shut him off, and then he was on the southern slope of the ridge, apparently intending to cut off the retreat of the In-

FORT PHILIP KEARNEY AND SURROUNDINGS, FROM ORIGINAL SURVEYS.

* Indicates block-houses in woods for working parties.
..... Dotted line, roads to Pine Island and Mountain.
— — Broken line, road to Virginia City, crossing narrow divide where bodies of Fetterman's command were found.
C, cemetery at foot of Pilot Hill.
☐ Corral, on road to woods, where train was attacked December 21st, 1866.

dians from the train. Wagons and ambulances were hurried up; the whole garrison was on the alert; extra ammunition for both parties was started, and even the prisoners were put on duty to give the guard and all available men their perfect freedom for whatever might transpire. Couriers were sent to the woods to bring back the train and its guard, to secure its support, as well as from the fear that the diversion of Captain Fetterman from his orders might still involve its destruction; and shortly Captain Arnold came to report that the whole force of armed men left at the post, including guard and everything, was but one hundred and nineteen men.

Until the wagons galloped out of the gate, we could see a solitary Indian on the highest part of Lodge Trail Ridge; but he soon disappeared. All this time firing was increasing in intensity, and in little more than thirty minutes,—after one or two quick volleys, the rattle of file-firing, and a few scattering shots,—a perfect silence ensued. There were then many anxious hearts, and *waiting* was perfectly terrible! The movements of Captain Ten Eyck were watched with intensest interest. The pickets could give no information, and a messenger sent upon Sullivant Hills could see neither Indians nor troops. It was just before Captain Ten Eyck's party reached the top of the hill across the Piney, north of the Virginia City road, that all firing ceased. Soon orderly *Sam-*

ple was seen to break away from the command and make for the fort, with his horse, on the run. He brought the message that the valleys were full of Indians, and that several hundred were on the road below, yelling and challenging them to come down; but nothing could be seen of Fetterman. As was afterward learned, this party was on the very field of carnage, and doubtless they were completing their robbery and butchery. It was after dark when Captain Ten Eyck returned, with forty-nine of the bodies, and made the terrible announcement that all were killed.

To a woman whose house and heart received the widow as a sister, and whose office it was to advise her of the facts, the recital of the scenes of that day, even at this late period, is full of pain; but at the time, the Christian fortitude and holy calmness with which Mrs. Grummond looked upward to her Heavenly Father for wisdom and strength, inspired all with something of her same patience to know the worst and meet its issues.

The body of Lieutenant Grummond had not been rescued, and there was some faint hope that stragglers might yet come in and break the absolute gloom of the tragedy by some explanatory and redeeming feature.

At last the wood train came in, having seen nothing of Fetterman, not even having heard the firing, or suspected any additional danger after repulsing their own immediate assailants. Imagination only can suggest how wide-sweeping would have been the massacre had any considerable portion of the hostile bands renewed the attack upon the train after the successful decoy of the others to inevitable destruction.

With the next morning came a meeting of officers, with universal disinclination, generally expressed, to venture a search for the remaining dead. The safety of any small party seemed doubtful, and the post itself might be imperiled by a large draft upon the garrison. But the colonel had made up his mind, and freely expressed his purpose "not to let the Indians have the conviction that the dead could not be rescued;" and besides this, the very men who had passed through the war without blanching began to form ideas of the numbers and barbarity of the Indians, which threatened to take away one-half their real strength. So the colonel informed Mrs. Grummond that he should go in person, and would bring home her husband. Captain Ten Eyck, Lieutenant Matson, and Dr. Ould went with the party. Long after they left, and they left with the cheerful Godspeed of every woman and soldier of the garrison, on a holy mission, the pickets, which were distributed on the line of march, indicated their progress, and showed that neither the fort nor the detachment could be threatened without such connection of signals as would advise both and secure co-operation whatever might ensue.

Long after dark, the wagons and command returned with the remaining dead, slowly passing to the hospital and other buildings made ready for their reception.

Lieutenant Grummond's body was found, and eventually accompanied us on our midwinter's march back over the plains.

A careful roll-call of the garrison was had, and the body of every missing man was found. Wheatley and Fisher were discovered near a pile of rocks, surrounded by expended cartridges, proving that their Henry rifles had done good service. All the bodies lay along or near a narrow divide over which the road ran, and to which no doubt the assailed party had retreated when overwhelming numbers bore down upon them. Captains Fetterman and Brown were at the point nearest the fort, each with a revolver shot in the left temple, and so scorched with powder as to leave no doubt that they shot each other when hope had fled. So ended lives that were full of pride and confidence in the morning. Captain Brown's repeated dashes, and especially his success on the 23d of September, had inspired him with perfectly reckless daring in pursuit of Indians; and only the night before the massacre he made a call, with spurs fastened in the button-holes of his coat, leggings wrapped, and two revolvers accessible, declaring, by way of explanation, that he was ready by day and night, and must have *one scalp* before leaving for Laramie, to which place he had been ordered. He had inspired Captain Fetterman, who had been but a short time in the country, and already had great contempt for our adversaries, with the same mad determination to chase whenever they could, regardless of numbers; and together they planned an expedition of a week's trip to Tongue River valley, with a mixed party of ninety citizens and soldiers, to destroy the Indian villages and clear out all enemies. Disapproval of the plan did not change their belief in its feasibility and wisdom; but here were eighty-one officers and men, and among them the veterans of a long war, utterly destroyed in their hands, only six or seven miles on the route to that same Tongue River valley.

This massacre proved the value and integrity of Major Bridger and his statements, and no less showed the wisdom of a settled policy not to precipitate or undertake a general war while there was but a handful of men at the post; and the army had not yet received such increase as could promise any considerable support.

A kind Providence spared many, and the line of road opened in the summer of 1866 was maintained. Other regiments have strengthened the garrisons, and a year of changes finds the Indians still numerous and unpunished, but with the line still maintained; while the fruits of the labor of 1866 are yet to be valued when that country shall be occupied and sufficiently understood. If the line be abandoned by its garrisons, as is probable, to give better security for the Union Pacific Railroad, and if its choice hunting-grounds be given to the Indians, who seem to have a right to them at present, it cannot be doubted that the work done will have its value, and Eastern Montana will ultimately perfect its communications with the Missouri through the field of so much struggle and duty.

CHAPTER XXV.

THE FUNERAL, AND BURIAL OF FOURSCORE AND ONE VICTIMS OF THE MASSACRE—COLD AND SAD HOLIDAYS—EXPEDITIONS ABANDONED—REINFORCEMENTS OF AUGUST YET BEHIND.

THE bodies of the dead were first deposited in the spare ward of the hospital, two hospital-tents, and a double cabin. Details from each company assisted in their care and recognition. Many gave their best uniforms, decently to clothe their comrades,—and the noblest traits of the soldier were touchingly developed as they carefully handled the mutilated fragments, drew out or cut off the arrows, and decently composed all for the burial.

A long line of pine cases, duly numbered, was arranged by companies along the officers' street, near the hospital, and as each body was placed in its plain receptacle, the number and name was taken, for the future reference of friends.

The detail to dig a grave for this great entombment was well armed, and accompanied by a guard; but so intense was the cold that constant relays were required, and the interment was not achieved until Wednesday after the fight.

Over the great pit, fifty feet long and seven feet deep, a mound was raised, and the dead were buried with a sad and solemn stillness that will long leave its memory with those who had souls to estimate the circumstances and lessons of that dire calamity.

As if Nature herself were shocked by the enormity of the Indian torture there inflicted, and would still the passions of all, or forbid their immediate indulgence, it so happened that from the very night of December 21st the winter became unmitigated in its severity, requiring guards to be changed at least half hourly, preventing out-of door inspections of the guard, and driving officers, ladies, and men to beaver, buffalo, or wolf skins for protection from the cold.

The relief, as they hastened to their regular distribution, presented no bad idea of Lapland or Siberian life. The tastes, workmanship, and capital of the wearers were variously illustrated in their personal wardrobes. A uniform cap being useless and hardly endurable, even with coat-cape fastened, hood-like, over the head, the soldiers had permission to suit themselves in respect of substantial comfort. Mittens that ended at the shoulder; buffalo boots and leggings nearly to the thigh; hats as tall as a Polander's, with bushy wolf tails *pendant;* and tippets, comforts, coats, and vests of skins made an odd style of uniform under the existing Regulations for the better government of the Army of the United States. There were, indeed, times when the smallest possible number of men were allowed to be exposed, and *these* only while the corporal could return to the guard-house and fresh relief might promptly follow up the same routine of constant change. Some were frosted in crossing the parade, some on their sentry platforms; and guard duty with keeping warm were the principal work of all who had no part in hauling water, cutting wood, the care of stock, or the issue of supplies.

The holidays were sad as they were cold. Lights were burned in all quarters, and one non-commissioned officer was always on duty in each building, so that in case of alarm there could not be an instant's delay in the use of the whole command. Each company knew its place and the distribution of the loop-holes; the gunners slept in tents near their guns, and all things were ripe for the destruction of assailants should any venture to attack.

The constant and drifting snow-storms soon so lifted their crests by the west flank of the stockade that officers walked over its trunks, and when a trench ten feet wide was cleared, the next snow or wind would fill it, as only snow can snow and winds can blow in that suburb of Cloud Peak, the home of perpetual snow.

The men themselves, who, at the October muster, looked forward to the holidays and December muster with glad anticipations, forbore all demonstrations usual to such a period, and sensibly felt the weight of the great loss incurred.

Of the sergeants who had distinguished themselves in the previous war, or had actively operated in the labors of 1866, nearly all of the most prominent had fallen: Lang, a martinet, trim, upright, and soldierly; Bissell, calm, mature, and carrying into his profession the sturdy habits of business which had marked his life in Chicago before a hasty indiscretion impelled him to the army; Smith, the pride of the mounted infantry; Morgan, and many others, deserve an enduring monument over their last resting-place no less than heroes of more exalted stations from more memorable battle-fields.

The whole garrison shared the gloom. Charades, tableaus, Shakspearian readings, the usual muster evening levee at the colonel's, and all the social reunions which had been anticipated as bringing something pleasant, and in the similitude of civilized life, were dropped as unseasonable and almost unholy. Present and exacting duty admitted no dalliance with pleasures that were at other times rational and refreshing; and a calm, sedate, but genial sympathy brought most to a closer fraternity, almost confirming the sacred proverb, "That it is better to go to the house of mourning than to the house of feasting."

But no calm review, no wealth of language can bring before the minds of strangers to those scenes any conception of the realities experienced; neither would a literal catalogue of mutilations and outrages upon the persons of the fallen bring within the range of any imagination the capacity to present them as they were to the understanding of others. The aggregate of wrongs to single individuals would sum up the shocking features of many battle-fields; and the sum of all inflicted upon the entire party can have no precedent by which to estimate their horrors.

Nor was the abandonment of the proper recreation of the holidays the sole result.

Plans had been made looking to a short winter expedition, under the advice of General Cooke, that "three hundred infantry, with much suffering, could perhaps do more in winter than three thousand cavalry in summer." The exact method of doing this had not been settled upon, it is believed, though much talked of in social circles, where the ladies had the privilege of listening; and it was known that the colonel was determined, as soon as reinforced, to make such reconnoissances and outside movements as would test its practicability without risk to the post; but the destruction of Fetterman's command within a few miles of the post engendered doubts, which were freely expressed by the officers, whether the force that could be made available, even after a successful march and surprise, could entirely or signally destroy the villages of Red Cloud, with his warriors, his kniving squaws, and shooting papooses. Underlying these facts was the general congratulation that a successful maintenance of the post until spring should reopen the road to travel, would be a practical assurance to the Indian of the ultimate extinction of his hunting-grounds and the end of his supremacy in Absaraka. Others suggested that perhaps Red Cloud had concluded to keep himself vigorously awake, and try the surprise part himself, or so occupy himself as to consolidate all hostile bands into some comprehensive system of hostility to the post and the white man generally.

Besides this, it was a matter of notoriety and fact that, while the officers were anxious for repeating arms or breech-loaders, only old styles of rifles were on the way, and also that ammunition, not more than four or five months previously started from Leavenworth, was resting itself at some place not disclosed to the white warriors of Absaraka. Then the reinforcements had not come; and as the affair of the 21st, with the details of the same, had actually engrossed the time and energies of the whole garrison, the entire plan of destroying the Indians of the Northwest, while the mercury was motionless and the snow was all in motion, was temporarily dropped.

True it was that the spirit which drove Fetterman to hasty disobedience and certain destruction, viz., a desire to settle accounts for some of the outrages perpetrated during our six months' sojourn, had somewhat decidedly inspired all the ladies, as well as the officers and men, with a longing to do something explosive and brilliant; but the ladies had so often been told not to discuss military matters, and the tide of events having unfavorably settled the prospect of our husbands' gaining glory by miraculous adventures with Red Cloud, there was a quiet acquiescence in the condition of self-defense.

A stranger might have almost thought we were besieged. The commanders of Forts C. F. Smith and Reno so construed their condition; and the constant watchfulness, strict discipline, and ever-present preparation for all contingencies savored not a little of the same essence, as we passed the holidays of 1866-7 at Fort Philip Kearney, Absaraka.

CHAPTER XXVI.

COMEDY OF ERRORS—ENTERPRISE OF THE PRESS—TRANSACTIONS IN ABSARAKA MYSTERIOUSLY KNOWN TO THE PUBLIC BEFORE THEY HAD INFORMATION OF THE SAME.

Has any military event in history, whether sacred or profane, immediately after its occurrence called forth more elaborate and general explanation, and involved more contradictory and absurd criticism, all "founded upon fact," yet ignorant of that valuable article, than the massacre near Fort Phil Kearney, December 21st, 1866?

Of course the public could not be expected to know, nor the press to announce, that the only means of communication between that post and Fort Laramie, the nearest mail and telegraph station, was through two hundred and thirty-five miles of hostile country and through couriers sent by the post commander himself.

Neither could the great American people *wait* for information; but they must know exactly and fully all the particulars for perusal while coffee was cooling at the next morning's breakfast-table.

It was, of course, to be expected that the Illustrated Papers should act promptly and perspicuously, with all the embellishment and accuracy which wood engraving affords, and do this so truly to life that it would be at once recognized by all actors in its scenes; and it was equally certain and necessary that a "special artist," some "actual observer," or a "special correspondent," should furnish the editor's sanctum with the right material for his use in advance of the mails. There was certainly no difficulty as to historical precedents or illustrations of Indian warfare from which to combine a proper sketch, and accordingly the work was begun, even before the couriers had reached Laramie with details of the transaction itself.

As there was no one to contradict, and no one who knew the truth, a large margin was left for the play of the fancy, and the imagination was drawn upon with great freedom and success. The people were of course greatly shocked by the tragedy, and were certain that somebody was terribly to blame. The Indians were supposed to be so quiet and peaceful that nobody asked whether the massacre was one of a series; but statesmen as well as editors, those who claimed to know all about Indian affairs, and those who never saw a live Indian out of a city show, devised theory upon theory, to the great delight of their own complacent souls and with all the wonderful wisdom of absolute ignorance.

It could not be expected, in the urgent demand for particulars, that truth and justice would be the essential features of the whole; and the sensation had to be used just at the time, or somebody's paper or somebody's friend would suppose that somebody else, who was regularly compensated to cater to the popular passion for the startling and novel, was ignorant of that of which he knew nothing. So it happened that numberless journals *obtained, at last, the true version of that sad affair.*

Not to name those papers and thus arouse invidious distinctions where so many showed brilliant powers of imagination, a few choice selections will do honor to them all and injustice to none.

Albany, a city set on a hill, Argus-eyed and sagacious, had a corresponding pre-eminence in the way of invention and preciseness of detail. It portrayed, as *"from reliable information,"* the fearful climax, "when the last band of survivors were driven to the gates of the fort, knocking and screaming in vain for admission; when the last cartridge from revolver, carbine, and rifle was expended; when the sabers and butts of muskets were broken; and when, leaning against the gates, weary and bleeding and all resistance fruitless, all fell in one heap of mangled humanity, unsupported and uncared for." This sketch closed its recital with the startling announcement that the commanding officer, whom it doomed to future obloquy, with two full companies, was looking on, afraid either to fire or open the gates lest the garrison within should be massacred by the infuriated savages and the post should be sacked!

Block-houses, of course, reserved their fire! Loop-holes shone with the glaring eyes of frightened soldiery, but not with the gleaming rifle! Four howitzers, which could have swept the slope and bottom land, were silent and innocent of harm to anybody!

And yet, as a matter of fact, the fight was not within sight of the fort; and its capacity for defense or the support of any party near by was superior to the whole force of Indians in Tongue River valley.

One "Illustrated Paper" had a report "from the only eye-witness of the massacre." This person was said "to have been cut off from his party by Indians, and from a thicket only two hundred and fifty yards distant from the fight he saw the repeated charges of the cavalry, the dashing adventures of officers and men, and the last shot discharged by the last survivor through his own brain."

And yet, as a matter of fact, the very person accredited with this narrow escape and these providential aids to a close observation, did not see a shot fired by the party, or any part of the conflict; but went out with Captain Ten Eyck's relieving party, after failing to find Fetterman's party when firing was heard, and saw what Captain Ten Eyck saw of the fight, and that was —nothing.

A second "Illustrated Paper" had an engraving of the fight, and indicated in advance what should be done with the post commander. Others were hardly outdone by this. All had a convenient scapegoat for the whole affair. The gallantry and prowess of some were praised, while dereliction and cowardice were branded upon others.

Even the metropolitan papers of New York and Washington could not possibly wait, but discharged their shafts, regardless of character or truth. Thus pamphlets, letters, editorials, and pictures expressed their theories or positive statements; so that beyond the opinion of Lieutenant-General Sherman accompanying a soldier's letter, published at Washington in a pamphlet, with other documents sent to Congress upon the massacre, and a critique of the *Cincinnati Gazette* upon the pamphlet itself (author unknown to us), no correct account of the tragedy has ever gained access to the people at large.

To those who were present under the shadow of such a calamity, it seemed harsh and brutal that, more than two thousand miles away, there should be such quick and morbid ambition to citicise and abuse; and the ladies were not a whit behind the officers and men in thoroughly wishing that delegations from the eastern cities could spend some days in that country to try a few dashes after Indians, and take a turn at guard or picket duty, and live a time where newspapers are sometimes two months in coming, where bacon takes the place of sea-food, and desiccated materials put on the name and function of vegetables.

We had become perfectly accustomed and hardened to correspondents from the plains, whose warped or false representations discredited every good thing. Thus, for instance, three papers among those of the largest circulation in the country declared that the commanding officer was constantly giving powder to his enemies, and that ladies threw packages of sugar and coffee over the stockade to the squaws. A tenderhearted, sympathetic, but temporary attaché of the Indian Bureau knew just how the massacre occurred—viz., that the poor, hungry, starving women of the Sioux had come to beg, and their husbands had come to ask a little powder for hunting and to have an order revoked as to gifts of arms to Indians, and, being fired upon, they became desperate and took immediate vengeance. This critic, whose narration had its place on the tables of members of Congress, said a wood train could not have more than six men with it, and could not possibly have been attacked by three hundred Indians. He did not know how slowly six men would have built a post; nor that the timber trains sometimes numbered ninety or more wagons, each drawn by six mules; that each team required a driver; that the work required choppers and loaders and a guard to protect them; and that six men could not do this.

Some supposed that the whole was caused by ignorance of the Indian tricks and habits, and of the surrounding country, notwithstanding the fact that some of the officers not involved in the skirmish had spent the summer and fall in just such warfare and in reconnoissance of the country for miles in all directions.

Every conceivable hypothesis but the correct one was adopted, and everybody *guessed*, without seeming to think that possibly the authorities of the fort itself knew something of the affair, and were old enough to make some official report of the matter.

One said that the soldiers abused the squaws and the women of the country, although, except at the July meeting with the Cheyennes and the short stay of French Pete's rescued wife, there was never a squaw at the fort.

At least three disappointed aspirants for civil berths became newspaper correspondents and traducers; but the sting of their falsehoods was innocuous, as their inducement was understood.

One and all gloried in abuse; and no wonder is it that the hard labor of 1866, its skirmishes and exposures, its chases and its losses, were never told, lest credit should inure to the pioneer expedition to Absaraka.

The information supplied, and that manufactured, alike furnished some amusement to the garrison; but, for the sake of many friends who were anxious to learn the truth, it would have been grateful to the feelings had the truth been made known, to accompany the false as its antidote. At last the United States Senate called for the report of the commanding officer, at the April session, 1867, and again at the July session; and when it appears, some additional light may be furnished by which to confirm or disprove this comedy of errors.

NOTE.—Although Brigadier-General P. St. George Cooke removed Colonel Carrington from Fort Phil Kearney, without waiting for that officer's report, no sooner was that report received by Lieutenant-General Sherman, than General Cooke was himself relieved, and General Augur was assigned to fill his place.

CHAPTER XXVII.

NEW YEAR'S CHANGES—MARCH TO FORT RENO—FORTY DEGREES BELOW ZERO—HOW IT FELT AND WHAT IT DID.

NEW YEAR'S DAY, 1867, was without its anticipated festivities. All honor to the 27th Infantry,—until then the 2d Battalion of the 18th Infantry, and which on the last day of December severed its relations with the old regiment,— that during the holiday week they accepted their sad lesson, and with manly self-denial refrained from those indulgences which are so common at Christmas and the advent of a New Year.

On New Year's Day the Military Reservation was finally announced, in orders, giving to the burial-place of the victims of that great disaster a memorial character, honorable to the courage of the fallen.

A few days after, Brevet Brigadier-General H. W. Wessels, Lieutenant-Colonel of the 18th, a soldier with laurels and a gentleman without blemish, arrived with two companies of cavalry and four companies of infantry, of which one company was to be left at Fort Reno, his former post.

Orders came to remove headquarters to Fort Caspar, and all preparation was duly made. General Dandy, Chief Quartermaster, with discernment and courtesy, fitted up army wagons for the women and children, and deserves due thanks for our earthly salvation, as that preparation alone secured us a safe deliverance during the trip that ensued.

"After night cometh the morning," and at Crazy Woman's Fork, January 25th, 1867, the order of nature was regularly preserved. We left Fort Philip Kearney at half-past one P.M. of the 23d, just at the hour fixed. Packing had been done, wagons were loaded, houses had been evacuated for new-comers, and although the snow again began its fantastic drifting and plentiful resupply, the march had to be made, and the extinct road could hardly become more distinct, but possibly even worse.

By ten o'clock at night, by dint of shoveling and picking at proper intervals, nearly six miles had been attained, and the train corraled on a commanding summit to wait for the coming moon.

Lieutenant Bowman had been detailed to command the escort of twenty cavalry and forty infantry as far as Fort Reno, and discharged his trust with unwavering diligence and acceptance.

At one o'clock A.M. the bugle sounded, and just at three o'clock our invaluable guide and scout, Captain Bailey, reported "that himself and moon were ready." The sky had cleared, the stars were brilliant, and the aurora borealis faintly endeavored to show itself and cheer our onward way.

It is picturesque so to travel. Napoleon, it is reported, traveled over snow, but left his family; and the novelty of the movement of officers, their wives and children, and the usual families of band musicians, with their liberal allowance of future trumpeters, flutists, and drummers, gave this march a distinguishing feature not usually credited to that masterly winter trip of Napoleon to Italy by the way of the Alps. The wheels creaked, the mules made their usual vocal sounds at the early disturbance of their feed, and everybody shrunk into clothing as closely as possible to evade the increasing cold.

The thermometer hanging in our wagon allowed the mercury to do its share of shrinkage, and lingered about thirteen degrees below zero, with great apparent hesitation, if not positive reluctance, at being kept out of the bulb. Stalking in front, leading his pony, stamping through drifts and feeling his way, guide Bailey led off with inordinate self-possession, not to say coolness, and soon after daylight we were once more in camp at Clear Fork. Breakfast was soon over, the mules were fed, and the march proceeded. It was the remark of Captain Arnold that it was "*stunning cold*," and before twenty-four hours more were passed it became clearly evident that he had the right idea, and that expression will hereafter be to us not a provincialism of doubtful origin, but a *Simon pure* exponent of that style of cold.

Of course for awhile there was a keen watch for Indians, since as they see everything and know everything, it was just possible that they might envy us our horses, mules, and scalps; but the country was covered with buffalo, who did not even pay us the compliment of being scared, and in fact for twenty-five miles they were never out of view. Their quiet labor in the snow, wallowing and trampling for grass, was also a positive assurance, so said Bailey, that they had no red men in company.

So we plowed, dug, and plodded on. Before night we were at Crazy Woman's Fork. That any one of the party left it alive, and made the next march, now seems a wonder. The corral was formed in the grove at the bend of the stream, and wood was abundant after digging it out of the snow, but there a wood fire actually lost one-half its virtue. As fast as snow melted and rolled from the billets, which were heaped on as high as a man could reach, the same melted snow turned to ice, and each fire was soon girt about by constantly thickening ice. To stand fronted to the flame, then reversed, and to do this constantly that fearfully long night, was the resort of almost everybody. Cooking was out of the question. Hatchets broke our bread, and water was sufficiently warmed to thaw the chunks. *Slices* were not attempted. Thanks to our little stoves, the ladies essayed the luxury of *steeped*, not to say hot coffee, and with partial success. None of the special artists who portrayed the massacre accompanied us, but the picture of an entertainment given to Lieutenant Bowman, escort commander, and Captain Arnold, is still before us.

The general train formed a complete circle, with headquarters wagons in the center. By every fire were groups bending forward with outstretched hands to gather a little vital warmth. Hopeless of supper, most of the women and children closed themselves up in their wagons, and from each little stove-pipe the white smoke told all night how hopefully they were struggling to worry it through. Children were crying of cold, and men were multiplying expletives. Drivers left their teams, and began to avow that they "never would drive another rod until it was warmer." All at once the colonel and a party of officers approached our wagon and knocked. The door partly opened, and we know how it must have looked as a tin cup suddenly gleaming by the camp-fire was quickly delivered, and its recipient hastened to a blaze to imbibe its contents while yet unfrozen. Then another and another went out in the same careful way, and the door slammed again. Next, with the same caution, were passed forth bread, with pieces of the last turkey of Fort Phil Kearney, which, having been chopped with the hatchet, had also been softened over the fire, after the coffee had been concocted. As the door opened, we suppose the view must have been about as follows: In the foreground, a lady sitting upon a pile of wood, with feet to the stove, though these were covered with high buffalo boots, her head enveloped in a beaver hood, her form wrapped in linsey-woolsey and buffalo skins, and her hands stirring something like turkey knobs and bread chunks over the stove. In the background, in a perfect nest of wolf skins and beaver, two boys with caps, boots, and coats trimmed with the same material, and pushing themselves as close to that little sheet-iron arrangement as safety and culinary duties would permit; on the right and left a saber, shotgun, rifle, and revolver, with pendant pails and cooking utensils; at the extreme end, a thermometer, worn out and desolate.

The iron itself seemed jealous of doing any radiation whatever, and some dry pine wood which had been brought with us burned out so quickly, and lost so much courage and efficiency by constant replenishing, that it really was not the fault of the stove, for it could not possibly be heated through between times. It *never was red hot,* and its very top would neither thaw nor toast bread, unless when a kettle let down within had contact with the flame that struggled to do its best.

Lieutenant Wands, with indomitable tact and energy, was everywhere, between the necessary warnings, encouraging drivers, cheering up soldiers, keeping himself alive, and doing good generally. Everybody had some adventure. Mules got mad and broke loose, dashing just where they pleased, as if bound to keep up circulation by constant exercise.

Sometimes a party would be seen coming with a great log, struggling through snow nearly waist deep, and now and then some desperate character would throw himself down, determined to have a sleep if he froze to death. This was of course stopped, and with chattering teeth and aching limbs and benumbed feet, general stamping was resorted to, to keep circulation busy after the manner of the mules.

Mrs. Wands and Mrs. Grummond had the same school of practice in keeping up fires, and little Bobby Wands had the same ambition to burn his buffalo boots as other little boys we know of.

The convenient window in the wagon door, when the frost was scraped off, was a capital place for study of human nature under adverse circumstances; and it is morally certain that any one of those wagons, in the exact condition as then seen, would have been worth to P. T.

Barnum the restorative equivalent of his loss in the great fire.

At last the sentry called "one o'clock," and all through camp was reapted, "Good! it's one o'clock!" Some were for having reveille sounded at once; but guide Bailey, who had tried the ascent out of the bottom to the summit, eastward, found that no exit could be had until daylight. It was no doubt a lovely place for Indians, if they had been on that bluff, but they were not; and but for the shelter of the hill no living creature could have withstood the exposure.

From one o'clock to three, each hour was called, and at three the thermometer gave out entirely. The mercury settled in the bulb, froze itself stiff, and treated that sheet-iron stove with outrageous contempt.

FORTY BELOW ZERO! and the night dragged its hours *so* slowly! By four o'clock patience gave out also. Do or die was the impulse of all, and the slow work of getting frozen hands to put on frozen harness began, or rather such a thing was ordered to be done. Whether the teamsters thought the bugle summons was the thawing out of an old call, as once happened in the experience of the celebrated traveler Baron Munchausen, or they were too nearly frozen to appreciate their import, is not certain; but call after call failed to get them from their fires, until a verbal order, concise and to the point, promised all to be left behind, without wagon or rations, that were not ready to start punctually at six.

With the dawn came the report of the sad work of the night. Assistant Surgeon Hines had the fingers of both hands frozen, and they were already quite black; while many teamsters and nearly half of the escort were more or less frozen, some of them requiring amputations as soon as we reached Fort Reno.

With great difficulty, by the assistance of those comparatively uninjured, and the exercise of the positive authority of the officers, the train was at last ready. From the bottom land there was a sharp rise of nearly sixty feet to the bluff, and the first teams that tried it, even after the drifts had been shoveled away, repeatedly fell for want of foothold, and back came loaded wagons, dragging the kicking, tangled mules with them. Details of men took charge of the wheels, whips on either side, and ropes ahead, gave additional impulse; and in three hours the entire train had successfully passed the first sixteenth of a mile out of twenty-six to be made to Reno.

Just as the last wagons were buried in a deep cut, half a mile from the river, the alarm of "Indians" was given. A messenger came and reported that the rear was attacked. Teams were put to the gallop, the train was closed up, half frozen men in the wagons took their arms, and Lieutenant Wands, with a mounted party, dashed back to bring up the rear, and ascertain the facts. All proved a false alarm; but an hour was lost.

Fortunately the day was still and clear. The glare of the sun was at times blinding; but the goggles, which on the plains are used both against snow-blindness and dust, enabled all to get along tolerably well. Buffalo kept us company until within a few miles of Reno. Messengers were sent on in advance, and at dusk we safely passed its gates, and received at the hands of Captain Proctor, Adjutant Kirtland, and other officers, not only quarters, but all creature comforts for the whole party. Such was the first sixty-five miles march returning from Absaraka. Such were three days of our second winter on the plains. If we claim no special credit for endurance, and have never questioned the necessity of such a march at such a season, certainly, like good wives, we followed wherever led, and we do not envy any officer's wife, of however long experience, her claim to have had a harder trip after such a summer. Perhaps some have. Ours was ample for us.

It is now like a dream, when it comes to mind, that nearly one-half of more than fifty demonstrations of hostile Indians in the Mountain District were under the very eyes of the ladies of the garrison and their children. The lesson is not forgotten, as we no less recall the Mercy that spared us. Nor does a single sentiment of complaint or reflection upon the Indians, the *weather*, or anybody else, have its place in our recollections of the past. It was our impulse and duty to go, and we went. No regrets are entertained; but sometimes it seems that we should have had more enjoyment and quiet had there been more men along, and that the Indians would have treated larger numbers with greater respect; and sometimes it seems very strange that that trip to Fort Caspar, just then, was such a matter of life or death to the nation, as to make it a question of life or death to us.

CHAPTER XXVIII.

FORT RENO TO FORT CASPAR—THENCE TO THE UNITED STATES—COURTESIES OF THE ROUTE—VISIT OF DIGNITARIES, MILITARY, CIVIL, AND INDIAN, AT M'PHERSON—MORE CHANGES.

NEARLY three days were spent at Reno changing the infantry escort and providing for those who suffered. Lieutenant Jacobs, son of Dr. Jacobs, an old friend, at our birthplace, Danville, Kentucky, was its commander.

Our days' marches were *forced*, as far as snow would permit, and were—1st, Dry Fork of the Cheyenne; 2d, Wind River; 3d, Brown Springs, four miles east of the South Fork of the Cheyenne; 4th, the North Platte, near mouth of Sage Creek; 5th, Deer Creek Station, burned by Indians in 1865; and 6th, to Caspar. Indians had kept out of sight, and the headquarters of the 18th were again approaching a home. Lieutenant Wands, guide Bailey, and others rode forward, to give notice of our speedy arrival; when, all at once, we found our ambulance closed in by others, and upon looking out discovered the whole train on a trot, in column of six wagons front, and thus moving all in mass. The quick passing of an orderly was all that had been noticed, and without the sound of a bugle or other warning we found ourselves preparing for Indians, only six miles from Caspar. A party of red men had passed between the train and those who with Lieutenant Wands had gone in advance, and galloping close up to the telegraph office, had run off the stock of the horses just after the officers had dismounted at the fort.

The colonel, who was riding along a ridge somewhat in advance, recognized a mounted party crossing the Platte to be Indians, closed up the train and moved on; but pursuit was hopeless, as the Indians had seen the escort turn the hill in full view, and were nearly across the Platte three miles distant when discovered.

Soon we were met by Brevet Major Norris, a friend of old times, with his company of the 2d Cavalry, and returned with him to post, where he had already anticipated our wants. Here also Brevet Major Morris, Captain Freeman and wife, and Lieutenant Carpenter, all old officers of the 18th, competed in their welcomes, with other officers previously unknown, to us all. Here also, to our great delight, we met Mrs. Potter and her husband, the new adjutant of the regiment, who, after long service as acting assistant adjutant-general during the war, and as commandant of the District of Utah, while colonel of the 6th U. S. Volunteers, had been appointed to the 18th Infantry and at once placed on the staff. Mrs. Potter and little Carroll had just arrived from Laramie upon advices of change of headquarters.

The first thing done was to disencumber ourselves of blankets and furs. The next, was to open our eyes as Lieutenant Wands inquired where most would we prefer to go rather than remain at Caspar, the most barren and insignificant post on the plains. The apparent joke as to *preference* was earnest of a welcome fact; for sure enough, General Augur, upon assuming command at Omaha, had changed the headquarters station to McPherson, and thus we at once began to prepare ourselves to double our track to Sage Creek and extend our winter's march over the path of 1866, and within ninety-seven miles of old Kearney. Orders had miscarried, or the trip to Caspar would have been spared us.

The next day Captain Kellogg of the 18th, with his most estimable and lovely wife, arrived, and the associations of olden times were agreeably renewed.

Good-bys quickly followed, and with Brevet Major Morris of the 18th in charge of the new escort we were again on the way. The second day we reached the North Platte again, where Lieutenant Jacobs, who had now to return to Reno, bade his farewell, leaving pleasant memories of his courtesies as a gentleman and efficiency in charge of the escort.

Before stopping, on the sixth day of February, the colonel had the misfortune to be accidentally shot while riding rapidly to close up the train, by the discharge of his revolver, which had been badly repaired at Caspar, the ball entering the scarpal space, grazing both femoral artery and sciatic nerve, following the bone around to the outside of the limb, where it lodged. Instead of returning to Caspar, he ordered the train crowded forward to Laramie, and at noon of Saturday, the ninth of February, the corral was formed in the Laramie River bottom near the post.

The whole-hearted Mr. Bullock threw open his house, and, with Surgeon Shell, heaped upon the party that remained for twelve days with the colonel every comfort and attention that home itself could have furnished. The second day heavy snow fell, and the last of headquarters did not reach Fort McPherson until March 2d, although Adjutant Potter and Quartermaster Wands, with their families and part of the baggage, were sent a few days in advance. The trip from Laramie was without escort, none being attainable, although there had been an outrage perpetrated but a few days before between the post and Fort Mitchell; still, no danger was apprehended. The ride of fifty-three miles to the latter post was made in one day; and two or three days of rest passed delightfully, as Captain Hughes of the 18th, and Assistant Surgeon Cunningham, nephew of Lieutenant-General Cunningham of the British army, were our excellent and willing entertainers. They had given the same cordial greeting to the advance train, and thus Reno, Caspar, and Mitchell had alike kept up that old army hospitality which was once its pride and is the essential and redeeming feature of its isolated social life.

Scott's Bluffs, Fortification Rocks, Chimney Rock, and Court-house Rock, had a different language as they rose before us, cold and snow-clad; but even winter could impart no more gloom to their barren features; and the same cedars peeped through the snow that had dotted the sterile sides and cañons in the heat of summer.

Captain Neil, Dr. Latham, Mr. Adams and wife, and young Janney, of Columbus, Ohio, were still at Sedgwick, but otherwise few *old* friends were met. Brevet Lieutenant-Colonel Dodge of the 30th Infantry, which was in camp across the river, and Lieutenant Bennett also called. The sight of a full regiment reminded us how constantly General Wessels and the upper garrisons were watching daily for their arrival, and how long we had lived in the same expectancy.

The Platte was crossed on the ice; but it would hardly have been the fair thing to have passed it without recognition, so our ambulance broke through a few times, and three or four little scares were undergone for old acquaintance sake.

From Fort Sedgwick to Fort McPherson the drifting sands of summer had been overshadowed by the deep and drifting snows of winter; but with Valentine and Baker and Morrow to yield their best for our physical necessities, the journey soon came to an end.

We had been to Absaraka and back again! All phases of life, all eccentricities of climate and temperature, all grades of exposure and danger, and intercourse with all styles of human nature had been experienced or encountered.

Fort McPherson became home for a time. Here were some reminders of old times, as the spring of 1867 brought Indian depredations to the very vicinity. Here, too, were Indian councils, Indian visits, and Indian promises. Here, too, the Special Indian Commission spent a month in seeking interviews with the Ogillallas and Brulé Sioux of the Republican, and taking the testimony of Colonel Carrington as to the facts concerning Fetterman's massacre.

Here, too, a court of inquiry met to take testimony, and we had the pleasure of again meeting Captains Haymond and Phisterer, who left Fort Phil Kearney, August 1st, 1866, and had been summoned from Pittsburg and New York as witnesses respecting the affair of December 21st following their departure.

Here, also, were visits from Generals Sherman, Augur, and Custar; and here, also, Spotted Tail, Standing Elk, Swift Bear, Two Strike, Pawnee Killer, The Whistler, Long Bull, The Man that walks under the Ground, Joe Smith, Sharp Nose, and The White Antelope had talks, and gave pledges of friendship.

Here, also, the courtesy of Brevet Lieutenant-Colonel Mizner, of the 2d Cavalry, and his wife, and the officers of his command, and the sisterly welcome of Mrs. Potter made our arrival pleasant and our stay delightful, crowning with something like the amenities of old-fashion times in the States, our return from Absaraka, Home of the Crows.

But changes still occurred! Mr. Wands had been transferred to the 36th Infantry, and with his family soon returned westward again. Lieutenant Brent succeeded him as regimental quartermaster. Colonel Mizner took his turn to visit the Indian country farther west, and his accomplished wife anticipated our own trip eastward a few weeks. As at the outset so at the close of our trip across the plains and back again, the same kind Providence guided and guarded our footsteps, and more than ever brought home to the soul the sweet assurance of his presence

>Wherever we wander,
>Wherever we roam.

CHAPTER XXIX.

IN MEMORIAM.

THE dead of 1866, in the occupation of Absaraka, were those who were worthy. Officers and men alike had done duty well, and the majority had an honorable record before they engaged a new enemy in a new country.

Brevet Lieutenant-Colonel WILLIAM J. FETTERMAN, son of Captain George Fetterman, deceased, an old army officer, was born in garrison, and was instinct with the ambition of a soldier.

He was appointed a lieutenant in the 18th United States Infantry in May, 1861, and joined the regimental headquarters almost immediately. In the School of Instruction for officers, organized by the colonel of the regiment in July, 1861, he was ambitious and proficient, and in his duties as recruiting officer in Ohio realized substantial success, while, no less, commanding esteem by his refinement, gentlemanly manners, and adaptation to social life.

After he accompanied the regiment to the field, and when the changes incident to the war had placed the field officers of the regiment on detached duty, as generals of volunteers, Captain Fetterman commanded the detachment, and earned the reputation of being a brave soldier.

His return to the regiment in November, 1866, had been sought, and no less looked for with glad anticipation, as officers were so few, and his social and professional character alike made him a favorite.

As the senior officer serving with the 2d Battalion, just taking the new style of the 27th Infantry, it was naturally expected that he would take command of it whenever the colonel should join the 1st Battalion, which was to retain the old number, but had its companies on the lower route.

That he was impatient because Indians were not summarily punished, and permitted this feeling and contempt of the enemy to drive him to hopeless ruin, where a simple deference to the orders and known policy of his commander, and still higher authority would have brought no loss of life whatever, is matter of history; yet, such was the esteem entertained for him by his colonel and many friends, that as the grave received his remains, and the battle-field evinced the vigor of his desperate defense, no bitter reflections mingle with the necessity of rendering equal justice to the living.

In the prime of manhood and the pride of a noble spirit, he reached forth for laurels that were beyond his reach; and with all the support that human energy and quick haste could furnish, the error could not be retrieved, and his brief Indian campaign and life closed together, when he had just reached his new field of labor, inexperienced in its methods and contingencies, and incurring the saddest penalty for neglect of the experience of others.

In life he was a gentleman. In death he was mourned and honored.

Captain FREDERICK H. BROWN, enlisted in the 18th Infantry at Columbus, Ohio, was at once appointed a sergeant at regimental headquarters, and then quartermaster sergeant. Among the first appointments from the ranks, under the then existing law requiring the colonel to fill the vacancies of second lieutenant, Mr. Brown was second. He was almost immediately appointed regimental quartermaster and commissary, as his antecedent experience in the commission business at Toledo had peculiarly fitted him for such duty. This office, in the field and out of it, he filled until promoted captain, late in 1866, when he received orders to join his company at Fort Laramie.

He had become so attached to the country about Fort Philip Kearney, and so enthused by his purpose to take the scalp of "Red Cloud," that Indian skirmishing fastened itself upon his nature with the hold of some constitutional disease.

With it all he felt a deep sense of neglect that the flood of brevets which rolled over the regiment omitted his name; and when one officer was breveted for services in the Atlanta campaign, although, during the whole period, that officer was at the North, and others had honors for similar erroneously designated services, he became impatient, eager, and reckless.

His intimacy in the family of the writer brought forth frequent sketches of his history and disappointments; and while he could cheerfully accept and reason upon the circumstances of the command, and intellectually recognize the impossibility of doing more than was being done to punish the savages, his restless spirit would hardly let him fill up the measure of his necessary duty, so set was his purpose to do some service that would command the recognition of his six years' of connection with the 18th Infantry.

On the night before his death, already adverted to, when he called, equipped for immediate duty, and at a time of the evening when there was no show for service, he was peculiarly earnest in his regret that he must leave without "Red Cloud's" scalp. He asked for the colonel, and said "he wished they would hurry up reinforcements. He was going to have one more fight if he had to work night and day to finish his papers." He adverted to the colonel's refusal to permit himself and Captain Fetterman to go to Tongue River valley on a trip with the mounted men, and said "he knew it was impossible, but he just felt that he could kill a dozen himself."

Those who knew Captain Brown, or, as all the officers styled him, "Fred," know how he overflowed with genial humor, and interested himself in whatever imparted social life to the march, or garrison life. His relation of an Indian skirmish on the 23d of September was frequent; and just before his death he made up its history, which he said "showed one good fight he had with the rascals."

That *his* impulses led Brevet Lieutenant-Colonel Fetterman to disobey orders on the 21st of December, at the sacrifice of the whole detachment, is not questioned; and yet we have no heart for blame when the strength of his friendship, his pride in his regiment, his disappointment as to honorable mention, and his brave but false estimate of the spirit of the Indian, challenge so much of our regard as memory brings him back to us, as when we parted but a few hours before he left earth's scenes forever. He said "he would always keep a shot for himself;" and doubtless thereby saved himself from torture.

Lieutenant GEORGE W. GRUMMOND, who fell in the same memorable slaughter, had achieved success in the war with the rebellion as captain and field officer of Michigan volunteers, and was understood to have been breveted brigadier-general of volunteers before he ceased his connection with the Army of the Cumberland. Our narrative has shown how narrow was his escape on the 6th of December; and the sketch of Fetterman's massacre shows how closely he obeyed his orders to remain with Captain Fetterman. His ambition prompted him to volunteer to accompany that party, and the fact that his remains were found with those of Sergeant Lang and a few others, more than a quarter of a mile in advance of the other dead, indicates that he either was covering the retreat or was disabled and killed in a gallant defense. He had a soldier's spirit, and in social relations was genial and already esteemed by all. He alone, of the fallen, left a widow to mourn his loss, and his remains returned with her to Tennessee, where they received their final burial.

CHAPTER XXX.

OMAHA TO VIRGINIA CITY, MONTANA.

THE foregoing narrative has given the distances for the best *day-by-day* marches, and such facts as to wood, grass, and water as are of practical value along the route from the Union Pacific Railroad to Fort Philip Kearney.

The westward-bound traveler will find at Omaha such extensive supplies of merchandise and outfit, at the establishments of W. R. King & Co., Jewett & Ely, John M. McCormick & Co., Hurfords, Lehmen & Co., Stephens and Wilcox, C. F. Catlin, S. & A. B. Saunders, and fifty other grocery, hardware, dry goods, and stationery houses, that he will find himself not a whit at loss if he has reached that city without much antecedent outlay; while the Union Pacific Railroad regularly transports its burdens beyond the first spur of the Rocky Mountains, passing *en route* the wagon departure at Horse Shoe Creek, and again at Cheyenne, affording a comparatively easy route to Laramie and points beyond.

To those who travel with their own wagons and substance, this narrative gives many hints;

but the whole line from Leavenworth, or Nebraska City, on the south side of the Platte, has been temporarily impaired by the Indian encroachments, the westward tide of travel, and the natural laws of that advance. With no affectation of scientific research more than to collect such botanical, floral, and geological specimens as the circumstances of the march would permit and a natural taste for such study would prompt, our information from competent sources, in company, sets forth Southern and Middle Nebraska as full of promise. The beautiful farming lands back of Omaha will find their contesting claimants; while salt, building material, and indications of coal show that the State is capable of expansion and self-support with little extrinsic aid.

Beyond Nebraska, and apart from the accommodations of the Union Pacific Railroad, the ox and mule teams still hold supremacy, and for their benefit some further information is given.

The trip of Major James Bridger and guide Henry Williams in 1866, who were sent forward by Colonel Carrington to visit the authorities of Montana and survey the route, or shorten it and open a new route, furnishes many facts additional to those contained in the report of Colonel Sawyer, and their notes, somewhat abridged, are by permission freely used for our present purpose, with the confidence that this will always be an avenue for travel, though interrupted in the settlement of Indian questions for a time.

The following statement closely approximates the odometer measurement of General Hazen in 1866, and while this is twenty miles less than Colonel Sawyer's route, the course of travel adopted by Major Bridger confirms his opinion that nearly thirty miles more can be saved as soon as the government or emigration can safely operate and improve the road:

Fort Philip Kearney to Fort C. F. Smith	91 miles.
Fort C. F. Smith to Clarke's Fork	63 "
Clarke's Fork to Yellowstone Ferry	90 "
Yellowstone Ferry to Bozeman City	51 "
Bozeman City to Virginia City	70 "
Total	365 miles.

The first distance is divisible as follows:

Fort Philip Kearney to Peno Creek Branch	5 miles.
To North Bank of Peno Creek, with timber, grass, and water	7 "
To Second Crossing of Peno Creek, with same supplies	6 "
To Croosing of Goose Creek, with same supplies	4 "
To Brown's Fork of Tongue River, with same supplies	13 "
To East Fork of Little Horn River, with same supplies	17 "
To Grass Lodge Creek, with same supplies	15 "
To Rotten Grass Creek, with same supplies	16 "
To Fort C. F. Smith, Bridger's Cut-off	8 "
Total	91 miles

Between Tongue River and Little Horn River eight forks are crossed, the largest of which, "Colonel Kinney's Fork," is quite a stream of clear water, with nearly two feet of depth in the autumn.

Between Little Horn and Big Horn Rivers are nine small streams of constant water.

The Big Horn River is nearly three hundred and thirty yards wide, with from three to six feet of water, and is crossed by a substantial ferry. In 1866 Kirkendall's train lost a wagonmaster by attempting to ford it; but it can be forded, with some little risk to stock and merchandise, at a low stage of water. It is unsafe for strangers, and the ferry is indispensable to general travel.

Fort C. F. Smith, on the Big Horn River, was built by Brevet Lieutenant-Colonel N. C. Kinney, Captain of the 18th Infantry in 1866, and suffered less from Indian adventures on account of the vicinity of the friendly Crow Indians, and because it was west of the main hunting-ground of the Arrapahoes, Cheyennes, and Sioux. It is the last residence of white men until the traveler reaches Bozeman City.

Associated with Captain Kinney in the building of Fort C. F. Smith, and with wonderful vigor and patience resisting the effect of wounds and apprehended heart disease, should be mentioned Brevet Major Thomas B. Burrows. His father is well known as the veteran friend of education in Pennsylvania.

The second distance, before referred to, is divisible as follows:

From Fort C. F. Smith to Dubois Creek, a fork of
Beauvàis Fork of Big Horn River, N.W. by N.... 10 miles.
This stream is about fifteen feet wide. Road good
except the crossings of two small creeks, and
distant from the mountains about seven miles.
The timber is ash and box elder.

To North Fork of Dubois Creek, N.W. by N.......... 10 miles.
Road crosses small creeks and ravines, and is quite
bad. The stream is narrow, and eight miles
from the mountains. Grass good, and timber
for fuel.

To South Fork of Prior's River, N.W.................... 8 miles.
Road passes one long cañon, cutting the divide
between Big Horn and Rocky Ranges, crossing
several creeks, and in places quite rough. Grass
good.

To Ice Water Spring, N.W. by N........................ 15 miles.
At four miles is water in a small branch. At five
miles farther is Millard's Spring, with good
grass and water. This spring rises and flows
from a high, level prairie, four miles from the
base of the mountains, forming a branch of
Prior's River, three feet wide and twelve inches
deep. At six miles farther comes Ice Water
Spring, with good grass, but no timber, although
at Prior's River, two miles beyond, the timber
is abundant. Road is in many places quite
rocky. Ice Water Springs rise from a mound
in the prairie, supplying four small streams
which unite in a channel six feet wide and three
feet deep, flowing with great rapidity.

To Spring Creek, W.N.W............................... 8 miles.
    Road crosses Prior River and its four miles of beautiful valley, thence up the valley of Spring Creek, or North Fork of Prior's River. Here are many steep bluffs until the road attains the summit of the divide between Prior's River and Clark's Fork. Grass excellent. Only sufficient timber for fuel.

To Clark's Fork, nearly W............................ 12 miles.
    The road is good, and all prairie except two dry creek-crossings, which are not decidedly bad. Clark's Fork is here nearly one hundred yards wide, with a rich valley and abundance of grass and timber.

              Total..................... .... 63 miles.

The third distance is divisible as follows:

To Rocky Fork.. 7 miles.
    This stream is forty-five yards wide, about three feet deep, with good ford. Luxuriant timber and grass. Ten miles from the mountains.

To Berdan's Creek—Branch of Rocky Fork.............. 12 miles.
    Rocky Fork is crossed twice. Good camping-grounds are found every three miles. Grass and timber abundant.

To South Fork of Rosebud............................... 10 miles.
    Three miles up Berdan's Creek. Road rough until the main divide is reached, between this creek and the South Fork of Rosebud. Stream about fifteen feet wide and two feet deep, abounding in beaver dams. Grass good; but only sufficient timber for fuel. Road runs six miles from mountains.

To Rosebud River Camp................................... 8 miles.
    Down South Fork of Rosebud one mile; thence crossing a divide of three miles. Rosebud is nearly twenty-five yards wide and two and one-

half feet deep. Cottonwood and willow timber is plentiful, and grass good. Thence down Rosebud four miles to best camp. About ten miles from the mountains.

To Stillwater, W.S.W.. 6 miles.

Road crosses the main Rosebud and follows up Stillwater Fork of Rosebud. Road good, timber heavy, and grass good. Stream is about sixty-five yards wide, three feet deep, and quite a rocky ford. About six miles from the mountains.

To Emmil's Fork.. 18 miles.

The road runs W.S.W., to North Fork of the Stillwater. Grass and timber very heavy, and camping-grounds every three miles. One divide is crossed before reaching Emmil's Fork, which here empties into the Yellowstone River. Emmil's Fork, named from the massacre of Emmil's party, in 1822, is about twenty feet wide and eighteen inches deep. The Yellowstone is here about one hundred and twenty yards wide and from three to five feet deep. The valley is from six to fifteen miles wide, and timber is very heavy.

To Big Boulder Creek... 17 miles.

Eight miles up Yellowstone valley, crossing "Lower Cross Creek" at five miles, and "Upper or Big Cross Creek" three miles beyond. Road, grass, and timber good; thence the road is over level prairie nine miles, with abundance of grass and timber.

To Yellowstone Ferry... 12 miles.

Road good. Timber is mostly on the north bank. The ferry is diagonally across the river, of nearly two hundred and seventy-five yards.

Total.. 90 miles.

The fourth distance is divisible as follows:

Yellowstone Ferry to Warm Spring, S.W.............. 4½ miles.
Up the Yellowstone River, after crossing, four and a half miles. Road here bears west toward the hills, becoming very heavy, and crossing a succession of small creeks and ravines.

To Twenty-five Yard River.................................... 10½ miles.
Southwest five miles across the ridge to the Yellowstone. Road difficult, crossing sidling hills. Up the valley two miles to foot of "Big Hill." Across the ridge, with better road, 3½ miles. This river derives its name from its width. Plenty of young timber, and grass good.

To Beaver or Pass Creek....................................... 17 miles.
Road runs S.W. by S. Road for ten miles very good, until leaving the river and entering the pass called Flat Head or Clarke's Pass. The last eight miles crosses a number of spring creeks, which flow from the snow range. No timber in this pass, except small pine and aspen.

To Cold Spring Creek.. 10 miles.
Up Beaver or Pass Creek. Road very rough. Grass good. Timber in abundance, of small varieties of pine and aspen.

To Head-waters, Cold Spring Creek....................... 5 miles.
Road crosses the divide to the east Branch of Gallatin River. Timber largely destroyed by fire several years ago.

To Bozeman City.. 4 miles.
Down the East Gallatin River. Here is a successful flour-mill, and a small but thrifty village.
Total.. 51 miles.

The fifth distance is divisible as follows. Road adopted in 1866:

To Madison River... 33 miles.
    Southwest to West Gallatin River thirteen miles. Road runs across the valley, which is twelve miles, and nearly all occupied by farms, with abundance of grass, and well watered by small streams from the mountains. This river is about one hundred and fifty yards wide, and from two to two and one-half feet deep, very swift, with a heavy growth of cottonwood timber. Thence, southwest by south, nearly twenty miles across the dividing ridge to the Madison River. Road good; grass abundant; but little timber near the road.

To Meadow Creek... 21 miles.
    Road crosses Madison River. This river is nearly two hundred yards wide and three feet deep. Thence up the stream five miles, westward up a cañon four miles, to main divide of Hot Spring valley. This spring boils up vigorously, and with temperature unpleasant to the hand. Near are the first quartz leads. The road is good, but rough. Thence south, across the divide, to Meadow Creek, twelve miles.

To Virginia City—by cut-off................................. 16 miles.
    The usual road is twenty-two miles.
              Total... 70 miles.

Aggregate distances 365 miles.

APPENDIX.

I.

THE following extract, from Senate Document No. 13, 1867, furnishes that portion relating to the massacre near Fort Phil Kearney in 1866, being Report of the Special Commission sent to investigate the cause of that disaster.

Disposition and Conduct of the Indians about Fort Phil Kearney, and the Causes of the same.

The main object sought to be secured by the treaty of Laramie of July, A.D. 1866, was the opening of a new route to Montana from Fort Laramie, *via* Bridger's Ferry and the head-waters of the Powder, Tongue, and Big Horn Rivers. This country was occupied by the Ogallalla and Minueconjoux bands of Sioux Indians and the northern Cheyenne and Arrapahoe tribes, and the mountain Crows.

The region through which the road was to pass and does pass is the most attractive and valuable to Indians. It abounds with game, flocks of mountain sheep, droves of elk and deer, and herds of buffalo range through and live in this country, and the Indians with propriety call it their last best hunting-grounds. All these Indians were reluctant to allow the proposed road to pass through these hunting-grounds, but all would reluctantly assent to this for so liberal an equivalent as the government was ready to give. The Indians were required further to stipulate that the government should have the right to establish one or more military posts on this road in their country. All the Indians occupying it refused thus to stipulate, and through the chiefs, headmen, and soldiers protested against the establishment of any military post on their hunting-grounds along that road north of Fort Reno.

While negotiations were going on with Red Cloud and their leading chiefs to induce them to yield to the government the right to peaceably establish these military posts, which right they persistently refused to yield, saying that it was asking too much of their people—asking all they had—for it would drive away all the game, Colonel H. B. Carrington, 18th United States Infantry, with about seven hundred officers and men, arrived at Laramie, en route to their country to establish and occupy military posts along the Montana road, pursuant to General Orders No. 33, Headquarters Department of the Missouri, March 10, 1866, Major-General Pope commanding. The destination and purpose of Colonel Carrington and his command were communicated to their chiefs. They seemed to construe this as a determination on the part of the government to occupy their country by military posts, even without their consent or that of their people, and as soon as practicable withdrew from the council with their adherents, refusing to accept any presents from the commission, returned to their country, and with a strong force of warriors commenced a vigorous and relentless war against all whites who came into it, both citizens and soldiers.

Quite a large number of Indians, who did not occupy the country along this road, were anxious to make a treaty and remain at peace. Some of this class had for a long time resided near Fort Laramie. Others (Brulès) occupied the White Earth River valley and the Sand Hills south of that river.

The commissioners created and appointed several of the

leading warriors of these Indians chiefs, viz., Big Mouth, Spotted Tail, Swift Bear, and Two Strikes. A portion of these Indians have remained near Fort Laramie, and a portion of them on the Republican fork of the Kansas River, and have strictly complied with their treaty stipulations.

The number of Sioux Indians who considered themselves bound by the treaty and have remained at peace is about two thousand, while the Minneconjoux and a portion of the Ogallalla and Brulè bands, the northern Cheyennes and Arrapahoes, with a few Sans Arcs, numbering in the aggregate about six hundred lodges, remained in their old country and went to war under the auspices of their old chiefs.

We therefore report that all the Sioux Indians occupying the country about Fort Phil Kearney have been in a state of war against the whites since the 20th day of June, A.D. 1866, and that they have waged and carried on this war for the purpose of defending their ancient possessions and the possessions acquired by them from the Crow Indians by conquest after bloody wars, from invasion and occupation by the whites.

This war has been carried on by the Indians with most extraordinary vigor and unwonted success. During the time from July 26th, the day on which Lieutenant Wands's train was attacked, to the 21st day of December, on which Brevet Lieutenant-Colonel Fetterman, with his command of eighty officers and men, was overpowered and massacred, they killed ninety-one enlisted men and five officers of our army, and killed fifty-eight citizens and wounded twenty more, and captured and drove away three hundred and six oxen and cows, three hundred and four mules, and one hundred and sixty-one horses. During this time they appeared in front of Fort Phil Kearney, making hostile demonstrations and committing hostile acts, fifty-one different times, and attacked nearly every train and person that attempted to pass over the Montana road.

Massacre of Brevet Lieutenant-Colonel Fetterman's Party, and the Causes which led to it.

General Orders No. 33, Headquarters Department of Missouri, dated March 10, 1866, directed that two new military posts should be established on this new route to Montana— one · near the base of the Big Horn Mountain," the other "on or near the Upper Yellowstone"—and designated the 2d battalion of the 18th Infantry to garrison the three posts on this route, and created the Mountain District, Department of the Platte, and directed the colonel of the regiment (Colonel H. B. Carrington) to take post at Fort Reno and command the district, which included all the troops and garrisons on this route.

General Orders No. 7, Headquarters Department of the Platte, June 23, 1866, directed that the 2d Battalion 18th Infantry should take post as follows: Two companies at Fort Reno, on Powder River, two companies about eighty miles nearly south of Reno, on the waters of Powder or Tongue River, which post should be known as Fort Philip Kearney, and two companies at the crossing of the Big Horn River on the same road, and about seventy miles beyond Fort Philip Kearney, to be known as Fort C. F. Smith, and directed that the colonel of the regiment should take post at Fort Philip Kearney, and command the "mountain district."

The orders above referred to were issued with the express understanding, apparently, that this road to Montana was to be opened through the Indian country by compact or treaty with the Indians occupying it, and not by conquest and the exercise of arbitrary power on the part of the government. Hence Colonel Carrington's instructions looked mainly to the duty of selecting and building the two new forts, Philip Kearney and C. F. Smith, and the command assigned was only sufficient for this purpose and properly garrisoning the posts. This command numbered in all about seven hundred men, five hundred of whom were new recruits, and twelve officers, including district commander and staff. The commanding officer, Colonel Carrington, could not and did not fail to see at once, that although his command was entirely sufficient to erect the new forts, build the barracks, warehouses, and stables, and make preparations for winter, and properly garrison his posts, and could protect emigration from the small thieving parties of Indians, it was still entirely inadequate to carry on systematic and aggressive war against a most powerful tribe of Indians, fighting to maintain possession and control of their own country, in addition to those other duties. This officer carried the orders above referred to into effect with promptness and zeal, organizing the mountain district June 28, 1866, establishing Fort Philip Kearney on the 15th of July, and Fort C. F. Smith on the 3d day of August, and as early as the 31st day of July informed General P. St. George Cooke, the department commander, that the status of Indians in that country was one of war, and requested reinforcements sent to him, and two days previously had telegraphed the adjutant-general of the army for Indian auxiliaries, and additional force of his own regiment.

On the 9th of August, General Cooke, commanding department of the Platte, informed Colonel Carrington that Lieutenant-General Sherman ordered the posts in his, Colonel Carrington's district, supported as much as possible, and announced a regiment coming from St. Louis.

No auxiliaries were assigned, and no reinforcements came until November, when company C, 2d United States Cavalry, reached Fort Kearney, sixty strong, armed with Springfield rifles and Star carbines. In December, about ninety recruits joined the battalion in the mountain district, a portion of whom were assigned to a company stationed at Fort Phil Kearney. No other reinforcements were sent to the district. Approved requisitions for ammunition were not answered. The command at Fort C. F. Smith was reduced to ten rounds per man; the command at Fort Phil Kearney to forty-five rounds per man, and the command at Fort Reno to thirty rounds per man. Recruits could not practice any in firing. Little time could be allowed from fatigue duty for drill, and with but twelve officers and three posts little could have been done in drilling recruits, if time could have been allowed.

The result of all this was that the troops were in no condition to fight successful battles with Indians or other foes, and this from no fault of Colonel Carrington; and I am astonished at the zeal with which they fought, and the damage they inflicted, December 21st.

The numerous demonstrations and attacks made by Indians prior to the 6th of December seemed to have been made for the sole purpose of capturing stock, picket posts, and small parties of soldiers who might venture beyond the cover of the garrison, and of annoying and checking the wood train constantly drawing material for the new forts.

On the morning of December 6th the wood train was attacked, a common occurrence, about two miles from the fort, and forced to corral and defend itself. Brevet Lieutenant-Colonel Fetterman, with a command of seventeen mounted infantry and thirty-five cavalry, moved out to relieve the wood train, and drive off the Indians, and Colonel Carrington, with twenty-five mounted infantry, moved out for the purpose of cutting off the Indians from retreat, and destroying them. On this day, at a point on Peno Creek, about five miles from the fort, the Indians, the second time after the fort was established, made a stand and strong resistance, and nearly surrounded Colonel Fetterman's party. The infantry obeyed orders and behaved well. The cavalry, with the exception of ten enlisted men, disobeyed the orders of Colonel Fetterman, and fled with great precipitancy from this portion of the field. As the cavalry retreated, the Indians made a great display and every effort to create a panic with the infantry, but Colonel Fetterman, Lieutenant Wands, and Lieutenant Brown succeeded in keeping this small body of infantry cool-

and by reserving their fire for proper range, rescued it from annihilation, and made a junction with Colonel Carrington's party, on the east side of Peno Creek. Lieutenant Bingham, after leaving Colonel Fetterman's party, with Lieutenant Grummond, a sergeant from Colonel Carrington's command, and two men from his own, without the knowledge or orders of any of his superiors, pursued into an ambuscade, more than two miles from the main party, a single Indian who was on foot just in front of their horses, and Lieutenant Bingham and the sergeant were there killed. The results of this day's fighting, although not of a decidedly successful character to the Indians, were such as naturally to induce the belief on their part that by proper management and effort they could overpower and destroy any force that could be sent out from the fort to fight them, and no doubt at this time resolved to make the effort the first auspicious day, and postponed their proceedings from the new to the full moon. In the mean time everything was quiet about the fort, although they often appeared on the surrounding hills.

On the morning of December 21st the picket at the signal station signaled to the fort that the wood train was attacked by Indians, and coralled, and the escort fighting. This was not far from 11 o'clock A.M., and the train was about two miles from the fort, and moving toward the timber. Almost immediately a few Indian pickets appeared on one or two of the surrounding heights, and a party of about twenty near the Big Piney, where the Montana road crosses the same, within howitzer range of the fort. Shells were thrown among them from the artillery in the fort, and they fled.

The following detail, viz., fifty men and two officers from the four different infantry companies, and twenty-six cavalrymen and one officer, was made by Colonel Carrington. The entire force formed in good order and was placed under command of Brevet Lieutenant-Colonel Fetterman, who received the following orders from Colonel Carrington: "Support the wood train, relieve it, and report to me. Do not engage or pursue Indians at its expense; under no circumstances pursue over Lodge Trail Ridge." These instructions were repeated by Colonel Carrington in a loud voice, to the command when in motion, and outside the fort, and again delivered in substance through Lieutenant Wands, officer of the day, to Lieutenant Grummond, commanding cavalry detachment, who was requested to communicate them again to Colonel Fetterman.

Colonel Fetterman moved out rapidly to the right of the wood road, for the purpose no doubt of cutting off the retreat of the Indians then attacking the train. As he advanced across the Piney, a few Indians appeared in his front and on his flanks, and continued flitting about him, beyond rifle range, till they disappeared beyond Lodge Trail Ridge. When he was on Lodge Trail Ridge, the picket signaled the fort that the Indians had retreated from the train; the train had broken corral and moved on toward the timber.

The train made the round trip, and was not again disturbed that day.

At about fifteen minutes before 12 o'clock Colonel Fetterman's command had reached the crest of Lodge Trail Ridge, was deployed as skirmishers, and at a halt. Without regard to orders, for reasons that the silence of Colonel Fetterman now prevents us from giving, he, with the command, in a few moments disappeared, having cleared the ridge, still moving north. Firing at once commenced, and increased in rapidity till, in about fifteen minutes and at about 12 o'clock M., it was a continuous and rapid fire of musketry, plainly audible at the fort. Assistant Surgeon Hines, having been ordered to join Fetterman, found Indians on a part of Lodge Trail Ridge not visible from the fort, and could not reach the force there struggling to preserve its existence. As soon as the firing became rapid Colonel Carrington ordered Captain Ten Eyck, with about seventy-six men, being all the men for duty in the fort, and two wagons with ammunition, to join Colonel Fetterman immediately. He moved out and advanced rapidly toward the point from which the sound of firing proceeded, but did not move by so short a route as he might have done. The sound of firing continued to be heard during his advance, diminishing in rapidity and number of shots till he reached a high summit overlooking the battle-field, at about a quarter before 1 o'clock, when one or two shots closed all sound of conflict.

Whether he could have reached the scene of action by marching over the shortest route as rapidly as possible in time to have relieved Colonel Fetterman's command, I am unable to determine.

Immediately after Captain Ten Eyck moved out, and by orders of Colonel Carrington issued at the same time as the orders detailing that officer to join Colonel Fetterman, the quartermaster's employees, convalescents, and all others in garrison, were armed and provided with ammunition, and held in readiness to reinforce the troops fighting, or defend the garrison.

Captain Ten Eyck reported, as soon as he reached a summit commanding a view of the battle-field, that the Peno valley was full of Indians; that he could see nothing of Colonel Fetterman's party, and requested that a howitzer should be sent to him. The howitzer was not sent. The Indians, who at first beckoned him to come down, now commenced retreating, and Captain Ten Eyck, advancing to a point where the Indians had been standing in a circle, found the dead naked bodies of Brevet Lieutenant-Colonel Fetterman, Captain Brown, and about sixty-five of the soldiers of their command. At this point there were no indications of a severe struggle. All the bodies lay in a space not exceeding thirty-five feet in diameter. No empty cartridge shells were about, and there were some full cartridges. A few American horses lay dead a short distance off, all with their heads toward the fort. This spot was by the roadside, and beyond the summit of a hill rising to the east of Peno Creek. The road, after rising this hill, follows this ridge along for about half or three-quarters of a mile, and then descends abruptly to Peno Creek. At about half the distance from where these bodies lay to the point where the road commences to descend to Peno Creek was the dead body of Lieutenant Grummond; and still farther on, at the point where the road commences to descend to Peno Creek, were the dead bodies of the three citizens and four or five of the old, long-tried and experienced soldiers. A great number of empty cartridge shells were on the ground at this point, and more than fifty lying on the ground about one of the dead citizens, who used a Henry rifle. Within a few hundred yards in front of this position ten Indian ponies lay dead, and there were sixty-five pools of dark and clotted blood. No Indian ponies or pools of blood were found at any other point. Our conclusion, therefore, is that the Indians were massed to resist Colonel Fetterman's advance along Peno Creek on both sides of the road; that Colonel Fetterman formed his advanced lines on the summit of the hill overlooking the creek and valley, with a reserve near where the large number of dead bodies lay; that the Indians, in force of from fifteen to eighteen hundred warriors, attacked him vigorously in this position, and were successfully resisted by him for half an hour or more; that the command then being short of ammunition, and seized with panic at this event and the great numerical superiority of the Indians, attempted to retreat toward the fort; that the mountaineers and old soldiers, who had learned that a movement from Indians, in an engagement, was equivalent to death, remained in their first position, and were killed there; that immediately upon the commencement of the retreat the Indians charged upon and surrounded the party, who could not now be formed by their officers, and were immediately killed. Only six men of the whole command were killed by balls, and two of these Lieutenant-Colonel Fetterman and Captain Brown, no doubt inflicted this death upon themselves, or each other, by their own hands, for both were shot through the left temple, and powder burnt into the skin and flesh about the wound. These officers had also oftentimes asserted that they would not be taken alive by Indians.

In the critical examination we have given this painful and horrible affair, we do not find, of the immediate participants, any officer living deserving of censure; and even if evidence justifies it, it would ill become us to speak evil of or censure those dead who sacrificed life struggling to maintain the authority and power of the government and add new luster to our arms and fame.

Of those who have been more remotely connected with the events that led to the massacre, we have endeavored to report so specifically as to enable yourself and the President, who have much official information that we cannot have, to determine where the censure must fall. The difficulty, "in a nutshell," was that the commanding officer of the district was furnished no more troops or supplies for this state of war than had been provided and furnished him for a state of profound peace.

In regions where all was peace, as at Laramie in November, twelve companies were stationed; while in regions where all was war, as at Phil Kearney, there were only five companies allowed.

II.

SKETCH OF THE EIGHTEENTH UNITED STATES INFANTRY.

The 18th Regiment United States Infantry has served on the plains since November, 1865. During the fall of that year, the 1st Battalion, under Captain and Brevet Lieutenant-Colonel R. B. Hull, occupied the lower line from Fort Leavenworth to Forts Lyon, Obree, and Dodge, marching in the depth of winter, enduring great exposure, having at one time 85 men bitten by frost, and with reduced rations, being compelled to live for weeks on buffalo and other game of the country.

The regiment was commenced in July, 1861, and the three battalions were filled in little more than a year.

In November, 1865, the 2d Battalion, with headquarters under Colonel Henry B. Carrington, marched from Fort Leavenworth to Fort Kearney, Nebraska, where it wintered.

In May, 1866, the regiment again united, was again distributed on the frontier; and built, rebuilt, or repaired Forts McPherson, Sedgwick, Laramie, Caspar, Reno, Philip Kearney, C. F. Smith, Fetterman, Bridger, Morgan, Wardwell, Camp Douglass, and Fort Halleck, now Fort Saunders.

Up to January 1st, 1866, the regiment had received into its ranks four thousand seven hundred and seventy-three men, of whom three thousand one hundred and ninety were born in the United States. Of these, two thousand four hundred and ninety-nine were enlisted in Ohio, and of these, one thousand and forty-two were enlisted at Columbus, in that State.

Since 1866, seven hundred and ninety five recruits joined the regiment.

In 1867, the 1st, 2d, and 3d Battalions became, respectively, the 18th, 27th, and 36th Regiments, all of which continue on the plains in 1868.

The regiment lost in action, during the war, a total of nine hundred and sixty-eight officers and men, and has served in the States of *Ohio, Kentucky, Tennessee, Georgia, Mississippi, Alabama, West Virginia, Missouri, Kansas,* and *Nebraska,* and the Territories of *Colorado, Dakota, Utah,* and *Montana.*

The regiment participated in the following battles, besides minor engagements: viz.: "Siege of Corinth," "Chaplin Hill," "Murfreesboro'," "Perryville," "Jonesboro'," "Hoover's Gap," "Chickamauga," "Siege of Chattanooga," 'Mission Ridge," "Resaca," and the Atlanta campaign until the fall of that city.

One company, under Captain Ten Eyck and Lieutenant Kirtland, *en route* to join the regiment, participated in the siege of Mumfordsville, and was there captured, at the surrender of the post to overwhelming numbers,—General Bragg's entire army having laid siege to the post.

The regiment was with Colonel Robert McCook at the battle of Mill Springs, to whom Colonel Carrington turned over the command of his brigade, consisting of the 9th and 35th Ohio, the 2d Minnesota, and 18th Infantry, under orders to return to Ohio to complete the regiment.

At "Greysville, Ga.," "Tunnel Hill, Ga.," "New Hope Chapel," "Peach Tree Creek," "Kenesaw Mountain," and "Smyrna Creek," it had spirited encounters with the enemy; and before the cedars at "Stone River," lost in less than an hour two hundred and ninety-eight men, nearly half the force engaged.

During the war it marched on foot 2447 miles; by railroad, 483 miles; by water, 1948 miles, being a total of 4878 miles.

The following is the list of officers assigned to the regiment from its first organization, with the changes that have occurred, and the present status of such as remain in the Army in 1868:

Henry B. Carrington, Colonel, May 14, 1861. Colonel 18th Infantry in 1868.

*Oliver L. Shepherd, Lieutenant-Colonel, May 14, 1861. Colonel 15th Infantry in 1868.

*Charles S. Lovell, Lieutenant-Colonel, January 7, 1863. Colonel 14th Infantry in 1868.

*Henry W. Wessells, Lieutenant-Colonel, February 16, 1865. Lieutenant-Colonel 18th Infantry in 1868.

Frederick Townsend, Major, May 14, 1861. Lieutenant-Colonel 9th Infantry in 1868.

*Henry Burton, Major, May 14, 1861. Declined promotion from 3d Artillery.

Edmund Underwood, Major, May 14, 1861. Retired in 1862.

William A. Stokes, Major, September 7, 1861. Not confirmed.

*James N. Caldwell, Major, February 27, 1862. Retired in 1863.

*W. T. H. Brooks, Major, March 12, 1862. Resigned July 14th, 1864.

*James Van Voast, Major, December 29, 1863. Major 18th Infantry in 1868.

*Charles R. Wood, Major, April 20, 1864. Lieutenant-Colonel 33d Infantry in 1868.

*William H. Lewis, Major, July 14, 1864. Major 36th Infantry in 1868.

*Henry Douglass, Captain, May 14, 1861. Major 3d Infantry in 1868.

*Thomas M. Vincent, Captain, May 14, 1861. Declined promotion from 2d Artillery.

*Alexander Chambers, Captain, May 14, 1861. Major 22d Infantry in 1868.

*Alexander Piper, Captain, May 14, 1861. Declined promotion from 3d Artillery.

APPENDIX. 273

Henry R. Mizner, Captain, May 14, 1861. Captain 36th Infantry in 1868.

*Thomas C. Sullivan, Captain, May 14, 1861. Declined promotion from 1st Artillery.

Jacob W. Eyster, Captain, May 14, 1861. Out of service February 15, 1865.

William S. Thrustin, Captain, May 14, 1861. Resigned August 12, 1863.

William M. McGlaughlin, Captain, May 14, 1861. Declined appointment.

Charles E. Dennison, Captain, May 14, 1861. Wounded at Stone River. Died January 15, 1863.

*Platt J. Titus, Captain, May 14, 1861. Declined appointment.

Henry R. Belknap, Captain, May 14, 1861. Resigned May 30, 1863.

Alvah H. Bereman, Captain, May 14, 1861. Resigned July 22, 1862.

Moses M. Granger, Captain, May 14, 1861. Resigned May 30, 1862.

David L. Wood, Captain, May 14, 1861. Wholly retired September 11, 1863.

Patrick H. Breslin, Captain, May 14, 1861. Out of service November 25, 1862.

*Lyman M. Kellogg, Captain, May 14, 1861. Captain 18th Infantry in 1868.

Jacob Weidenkopf, Captain, August 5, 1861. Declined appointment.

A. B. Thompson, Captain, August 5, 1861. Retired May 6, 1864.

George W. Smith, Captain, August 5, 1861. Resigned in 1866.

John A. Thompson, Captain, October 26, 1861. Wounded at Hoover's Gap. Died June 30, 1863.

Henry Haymond, Captain, October 26, 1861. Captain 27th Infantry in 1868.

John H. Knight, Captain, August 20, 1861. Captain 36th Infantry in 1868.

Philip R. Forney, Captain, February 9, 1862. Transferred to 9th Infantry in 1866.

Tenodor Ten Eyck, Captain, February 19, 1862. Captain 18th Infantry in 1868.

Mark F. Leavenworth, Captain, February 19, 1862. Resigned April 27, 1863.

*James W. Forsyth, First Lieutenant, March 15, 1861. Major 10th Cavalry in 1868.

*William B. Hughes, First Lieutenant, April 1, 1861. Declined transfer from 9th Infantry.

*Francis J. Crilly, First Lieutenant, May 14, 1861. Declined promotion from 7th Infantry.

*Elisha E. Camp, First Lieutenant, May, 14, 1861. Declined promotion from 9th Infantry.

Robert B. Hull, First Lieutenant, May 14, 1861. Captain 18th Infantry in 1868.

William J. Fetterman, First Lieutenant, May 14, 1861. Captain, killed in action with Indians near Fort Phil Kearney, December 21, 1866.

Charles L. Kneass, First Lieutenant, May 14, 1861. Captain, killed at Stone River, December 31, 1862.

Andrew D. Cash, Jr., First Lieutenant, May 14th, 1861. Died at Louisville, Ky., March 24, 1862.

Ansel B. Denton, First Lieutenant, May 14, 1861. Resigned while Captain, September 9th, 1864.

William H. H. Taylor, First Lieutenant, May 14, 1861. Resigned September 12, 1863.

Nathanial C. Kinney, First Lieutenant, May 14, 1861. Captain, and resigned in 1867.

Richard L. Morris, Jr., First Lieutenant, May 14, 1861. Captain 18th Infantry in 1868.

Joseph L. Proctor, First Lieutenant, May 14, 1861. Captain 27th Infantry in 1868.

Anson Mills, First Lieutenant, May 14, 1861. Captain 18th Infantry in 1868.

APPENDIX. 275

Andrew S. Burt, First Lieutenant, May 14, 1861. Captain 27th Infantry in 1868.

Thomas B. Burrows, First Lieutenant, May 14, 1861. Captain 27th Infantry in 1868.

*Symmes Gardner, First Lieutenant, May 14, 1861. Dropped November 13, 1863.

Claudius Schmidt, First Lieutenant, May 14, 1861. Resigned June 30, 1862.

Morgan L. Ogden, First Lieutenant, May 14, 1861. Captain 18th Infantry in 1868.

Wm. W. Stevenson, First Lieutenant, May 14, 1861. Died at Louisville, Ky., February 27, 1862.

Thomas F. Brand, First Lieutenant, May 14, 1861. Retired as Captain December 31, 1864.

James P. W. Neil, First Lieutenant, May 14, 1861. Captain 36th Infantry in 1868.

Herman G. Radcliff, First Lieutenant, May 14, 1861. Died at Murfreesboro', March 22, 1863.

John W. Hamilton, First Lieutenant, May 14, 1861. Not confirmed.

William O'Brien, First Lieutenant, May 14, 1861. Not confirmed.

Robert Sutherland, First Lieutenant, August 5, 1861. Resigned January 7, 1864.

William J. Phelps, Second Lieutenant, October 24, 1861. Declined appointment.

Horace Brown, First Lieutenant, October 26, 1861. Resigned July 28, 1864.

Irwin J. Wallace, First Lieutenant, October 26, 1861. Died at Pittsburg, Pa., February 19, 1862.

Charles L. Truman, First Lieutenant, March 6, 1862. Killed at Chickamauga, September 30, 1863.

Charles O. Howard, Captain, May 12, 1862. Resigned in 1865.

James Simons, Second Lieutenant, May 14, 1861. First Lieutenant, died January 14, 1863, of wounds received at Stone River.

James Powell, Second Lieutenant, May 14, 1861. Captain 27th Infanty, and retired in 1868.

Wm. P. McCleery, Second Lieutenant, May 14, 1861. Captain 18th Infantry in 1868.

Daniel W. Benham, Second Lieutenant, October 24, 1861. Captain 36th Infantry in 1868.

Frederick Phisterer, Second Lieutenant, October 30, 1861. Captain 36th Infantry in 1868.

Frederick H. Brown, Second Lieutenant, October 30, 1861. Captain, killed in action with Indians near Fort Phil Kearney, December 21, 1866.

Henry B. Freeman, Second Lieutenant, October 30, 1861. Captain 27th Infantry in 1868.

Samuel J. Dick, Second Lieutenant, October 30, 1861. Died at Nashville, December 24, 1864.

James P. Galloway, Second Lieutenant, October 30, 1861. Not confirmed.

Thaddeus S. Kirtland, Second Lieutenant, October 30, 1861. Captain 36th Infantry in 1868.

Joseph McConnell, Second Lieutenant, October 30, 1861. First Lieutenant, died January 14, 1863, of wounds received at Stone River.

James E. Mitchel, Second Lieutenant, February 19, 1862. Died of disease.

Gilbert S. Carpenter, Second Lieutenant, June 9, 1862. Captain 45th Infantry in 1868.

William H. Bisbee, Second Lieutenant, June 9, 1862. Captain 27th Infantry in 1868.

Merrill N. Hutchinson, Second Lieutenant, June 9, 1862. Retired as First Lieutenant.

Ebenezer D. Harding, Second Lieutenant, June 9, 1862. Captain, and retired wholly.

John F. Hitchcock, Second Lieutenant, June 9, 1862. Killed at Stone River, December 31, 1862.

Augustus A. Meckling, Second Lieutenant, June 9, 1862. Resigned December 24, 1862.

APPENDIX. 277

Lucius F. Brown, Second Lieutenant, June 19, 1862. First Lieutenant, died October 12, 1863, of wounds received at Chicamauga.

John J. Adair, Second Lieutenant, July 14, 1862. Captain, resigned in 1867.

Henry G. Litchfield, Second Lieutenant, July 14, 1862. First Lieutenant 36th Infantry in 1868.

Alfred Townsend, Second Lieutenant, November 10, 1862. Retired as First Lieutenant.

Charles Whiteacre, Second Lieutenant, November 19, 1862. Dismissed.

Wilbur F. Arnold, Second Lieutenant, November 21, 1862. Captain 41st Infantry in 1868, and deceased.

Reuben F. Little, Second Lieutenant, February 19, 1863. Resigned in 1864.

John J. Lind, Second Lieutenant, February 19, 1863. Resigned October 12, 1864.

Edgar N. Wilcox, Second Lieutenant, February 19, 1863. Captain 18th Infantry in 1868

Samuel C. Williamson, Second Lieutenant, February 19, 1863. Retired as First Lieutenant.

James S. Ostrander, Second Lieutenant, February 19, 1863. Resigned September 30, 1864.

Rufus C. Gates, Second Lieutenant, February 19, 1863. Resigned June 5, 1865.

George F. White, Second Lieutenant, February 19, 1863. Killed at Stone River before receiving his appointment.

William H. Madeira, Second Lieutenant, February 19, 1863. Killed at Stone River, December 31, 1862.

Frank T. Bennett, Second Lieutenant, February 19, 1863. Captain 42d Infantry in 1868.

David D. N. Corderoy, Second Lieutenant, February 19, 1863. Died before receiving appointment.

Orrin E. Davis, Second Lieutenant, February 19, 1863. Resigned October 12, 1864.

John Lane, Second Lieutenant, June 1, 1863. Died October 15, 1863, of wounds received at Chattanooga.

Isaac D'Isay, Second Lieutenant, October 31, 1863. Captain 27th Infantry in 1868.

John U. Gill, Second Lieutenant, October 31, 1863. First Lieutenant 36th Infantry. Resigned.

Henry C. Pohlman, Second Lieutenant, August 10, 1863. Died in Libby Prison in 1863.

William W. Bell, Second Lieutenant, February 21, 1865. First Lieutenant, killed near Fort Saunders, June 7, 1868.

William A. Stearns, Second Lieutenant, April 13, 1865. Resigned in 1866.

*Thomas L. Brent, Second and First Lieutenant, June 23, 1865. First Lieutenant 18th Infantry, and Quartermaster in 1868. Captain 18th Infantry in 1868.

*Wm. S. Stauring, Second and First Lieutenant, June 23, 1865. First Lieutenant 36th Infantry in 1868.

*Joseph K. Hyer, Second and First Lieutenant, June 23, 1865. First Lieutenant 18th Infantry in 1868.

E. F. Thompson, Second Lieutenant, December 14, 1865. Captain 27th Infantry in 1868.

Henry H. Link, Second Lieutenant, February 23, 1866. First Lieutenant 36th Infantry in 1868.

Oliver B. Liddell, Second Lieutenant, February 23, 1866. Resigned in 1867.

James H. Bradley, Second Lieutenant, February 23, 1866. First Lieutenant 18th Infantry in 1868.

Reuben N. Fenton, Second Lieutenant, February 23, 1866. Captain 27th Infantry in 1868.

George W. Wood, Second Lieutenant, February 23, 1866. First Lieutenant 18th Infantry in 1868.

Alex. H. Wands, Second Lieutenant, February 23, 1866. First Lieutenant 36th Infantry in 1868.

T. H. B. Counselman, Second Lieutenant, March 30, 1866. First Lieutenant 18th Infantry in 1868.

Winfield S. Matson, Second Lieutenant, April 9, 1866. First Lieutenant 27th Infantry in 1868.

Hugh G. Brown, Second Lieutenant, May 2, 1866. First Lieutenant 36th Infantry in 1868.

George W. Grummond, Second Lieutenant, May 7, 1866. Killed in action with Indians near Fort Phil Kearney, December 21, 1866.

Charles H. Warrens, Second Lieutenant, May 11, 1866. First Lieutenant 27th Infantry in 1868.

Oscar P. Hendee, Second Lieutenant, May 11, 1866. First Lieutenant 36th Infantry. Wholly retired.

Alvan S. Galbreath, Second Lieutenant, May 11, 1866. First Lieutenant 18th Infantry in 1868.

Jacob Paulus, Second Lieutenant, May 11, 1866. First Lieutenant 27th Infantry in 1868.

William F. Foulk, Second Lieutenant, May 11, 1866. First Lieutenant 36th Infantry in 1868.

E. A. True, Second Lieutenant, May 11, 1866. Declined appointment.

E. R. P. Shurley, Second Lieutenant, May 11, 1866. Second Lieutenant 27th Infantry in 1868.

William F. Davies, Second Lieutenant, May 11, 1866 Transferred to 36th Infantry and cashiered.

Jefferson P. Hibbets, Second Lieutenant, May 11, 1866 Declined appointment.

Sanford C. Kellogg, Second Lieutenant, May 15, 1866. First Lieutenant 18th Infantry in 1868.

Walter F. Halleck, Second Lieutenant, May 30, 1866 First Lieutenant 27th Infantry in 1868.

Joshua W. Jacobs, Second Lieutenant, June 28, 1866 First Lieutenant 36th Infantry in 1868.

C. H. Brewer, Second Lieutenant, June 30, 1866. Resigned 1867.

James Regan, Second Lieutenant, December 1, 1866. First Lieutenant 18th Infantry in 1868.

Wm. H. Campion, Second Lieutenant, January 22, 1867 First Lieutenant 18th Infantry in 1868.

Royal S. Carr, First Lieutenant, February 25, 1867. Resigned 1867.

Robert P. Hughes, Captain, July 28, 1868. Captain 18th Infantry in 1868.

James Stewart, Captain, July 28, 1866. Captain 18th Infantry in 1868.

Carroll H. Potter, First Lieutenant, July 28, 1866. First Lieutenant 18th Infantry, and Adjutant, in 1868.

Frederick F. Whitehead, First Lieutenant, July 28, 1866. First Lieutenant 18th Infantry in 1868.

Henry M. Benson, Second Lieutenant, February 23, 1866. First Lieutenant 36th Infantry in 1868.

William M. Knox, Second Lieutenant, February 23, 1866. Died en route to join regiment.

George M. Templeton, Second Lieutenant, February 23, 1866. Captain 27th Infantry in 1868.

Prescott M. Skinner, Second Lieutenant, February 23, 1866. Resigned 1867.

Charles E. Dibble, Second Lieutenant, February 23, 1866. Resigned 1867.

Henry E. Luther, Second Lieutenant, January 22, 1867. First Lieutenant 18th Infantry in 1868.

John A. Manley, Second Lieutenant, March 7, 1867. Lieutenant 18th Infantry in 1868.

William W. Daugherty, Second Lieutenant, March 7, 1867. Lieutenant 18th Infantry in 1868.

Robert F. Bates, Second Lieutenant, March 7, 1867. Lieutenant 18th Infantry in 1868.

George S. Hoyt, Second Lieutenant, June 18, 1867. Lieutenant 18th Infantry in 1868.

Hiram II. Benner, Second Lieutenant, June 18, 1867. Lieutenant 18th Infantry in 1868.

John H. Todd, Second Lieutenant, August 22, 1867. Lieutenant 18th Infantry in 1868.

Frederick H. E. Ebstein, Second Lieutenant, September 13, 1867. Lieutenant 18th Infantry in 1868.

APPENDIX.

The following officers have filled staff positions in the regiment, viz., as Regimental Adjutant:

First Lieutenant Charles L. Kneass; First Lieutenant James P. W. Neill; First Lieutenant Frederick Phisterer; First Lieutenant John J. Adair; First Lieutenant William H. Bisbee; First Lieutenant Carroll H Potter, Adjutant from date of joining regiment, and in 1868.

The following have been Regimental Quartermasters:

First Lieutenant James Simons; First Lieutenant N. C. Kinney; First Lieutenant Frederick H. Brown; *First Lieutenant Thomas L Brent; First Lieutenant Alvan S. Galreath.

The foregoing summary is gathered, by permission, from Captain Phisterer's Regimental History, and the Supplement of Lieutenant Potter, and affords to those interested in the incidents of this volume a more complete idea of the antecedents of the regiment, which followed up an eventful war record with scarcely less active duty since its close.

---

* Indicates graduates at West Point Military Academy.

NOTE TO APPENDIX II.

List of Men Killed in Action with Indians near Fort Philip Kearney, D. T., on the 21st day of December, 1866.

No.	NAMES.	RANK.	COMP'Y.	BATTALION AND REGIMENT.
1.	Augustus Lange........	1st Sergt.	A	2d, 18th Inf.
2.	Hugh Murphy............	Sergt.	"	"
3.	Robert Lennon..........	Corporal.	"	"
4.	William Dule............	"	"	"
5.	Frederick Acherman...	Private.	"	"
6.	William Betzler.........	"	"	"
7.	Thomas Burke...........	"	"	"
8.	Henry Buchanan........	"	"	"
9.	George E. R. Goodall..	"	"	"
10.	Michael Harlen..........	"	"	"
11.	Martin Kelley...........	"	"	"
12.	Patrick Shannon........	"	"	"
13.	Charles N. Taylor.......	"	"	"
14.	Joseph D. Thomas......	"	"	"
15.	David Thorey............	"	"	"
16.	John Timson	"	"	"
17.	Albert H. Walter.......	"	"	"
18.	John M. Weaver........	"	"	"
19.	Maximilian Dehring...	"	"	"
20.	Francis S. Gordon.......	"	"	"
21.	John Woodruff...........	"	"	"
22.	Francis Raymond.......	Sergt.	C	"
23.	Patrick Rooney..........	"	"	"
24.	Gustave A. Bauer.......	Corporal.	"	"
25.	Patrick Gallagher......	"	"	"
26.	Henry E. Aarons.......	Private.	"	"
27.	Michael O'Gara..........	"	"	"
28.	Jacob Rosenberg........	"	"	"
29.	Frank P. Sullivan......	"	"	"
30.	Patrick Smith............	"	"	"

APPENDIX.

List of Men Killed in Action, etc.—Continued.

No.	NAMES.	RANK.	COMP'Y.	BATTALION AND REGIMENT.
31.	William Morgan	Sergeant.	E	2d, 18th Inf.
32.	John Quinn	Corporal.	"	"
33.	George W. Burrell	Private.	"	"
34.	Timothy Cullinans	"	"	"
35.	John Maher	"	"	"
36.	George N. Waterbury	"	"	"
37.	Alexander Smith	1st. Sergt.	H	"
38.	Ephraim C. Bissell	Sergeant.	"	"
39.	George Philip	Corporal.	"	"
40.	Michael Sharkey	"	"	"
41.	Frank Karston	"	"	"
42.	George Davis	Private.	"	"
43.	Perrie F. Doland	"	"	"
44.	Asa H. Griffin	"	"	"
45.	Herman Keil	"	"	"
46.	James Kean	"	"	"
47.	Michael Kinney	"	"	"
48.	Delos Reed	"	"	"
49.	Thomas M. Madden	Recruit.	unas'd	"
50.	James Baker	Sergeant.	C	2d Cavalry.
51.	James Kelley	Corporal.	"	"
52.	Thomas F. Honigan	"	"	"
53.	Adolph Metzlers	Bugler.	"	"
54.	John McCarty	Artificer.	"	"
55.	Thomas Amberson	Private.	"	"
56.	Thomas Broglin	"	"	"
57.	William Bugbee	"	"	"
58.	William Cornog	"	"	"
59.	Charles Cuddy	"	"	"
60.	Patrick Clancey	"	"	"
61.	Harry S. Deming	"	"	"
62.	Hugh B. Doran	"	"	"
63.	Robert Daniel	"	"	"
64.	Nathan Foreman	"	"	"
65.	Andrew M. Fitzgerald	"	"	"
66.	Daniel Greene	"	"	"
67.	Charles Gamford	"	"	"
68.	John Giller	"	"	"
69.	Ferdinand Houser	"	"	"

List of Men Killed in Action, etc.—Continued.

No.	NAMES.	RANK.	COMP'Y.	BATTALION AND REGIMENT.
70.	Frank Jones...............	Private.	C	2d Cavalry.
71.	James B. McGuire.....	"	"	"
72.	John McColley..........	"	"	"
73.	George W. Nugent.....	"	"	"
74.	Franklin Payne.........	"	"	"
75.	James Ryan...............	"	"	"
76.	Oliver Williams.........	"	"	"
77.	John Wheatley..........	Citizen.		
78.	John Fisher...............	"		

Enlisted Men 18th U. S. Infantry........................49
    "   "   2d U. S. Cavalry...............................27
Citizens... 2
    Total 78

Names of Commissioned Officers of the 18th U. S. Infantry Killed in the same Action.

Captain William J. Fetterman, Brevet Lieutenant-Colonel U. S. Army.
Captain Frederick H. Brown.
Lieutenant George W. Grummond.

Recapitulation.

	OF'CERS.	SERG'TS.	CORP'LS.	PRIV'TES	CITIZENS	AGGREG.
18th Infantry..	3	7	8	34	....	52
2d Cavalry.....	....	1	2	24	....	27
Citizens..........	....	....	....	....	2	2
Total........	3	8	10	58	2	

www.ingramcontent.com/pod-product-compliance
Lightning Source LLC
Chambersburg PA
CBHW032108230426
43672CB00009B/1675